Praise for *Holy Conversation*

"More and more Christians are realizing that what people outside the faith need is not (a) a sales pitch, (b) an argument, (c) a sermon or (d) an information dump. Instead, they need caring, thoughtful conversation partners. If you want to become one, then there's no better starting place than *Holy Conversation*."

BRIAN MCLAREN, AUTHOR OF *A NEW KIND OF CHRISTIAN*

"A generation ago, Peter Berger's *Social Construction of Reality* observed that everyone is socialized into some specific worldview and that, in a pluralistic society—with many views of the world—the one intervention that most opens people out of their worldview and toward another is conversation with someone who lives by a contrasting worldview. At last we have a book for Christians that is immersed in this reality and teaches Christians how to cooperate with it."

GEORGE G. HUNTER, DISTINGUISHED PROFESSOR OF EVANGELIZATION, SCHOOL OF WORLD MISSION AND EVANGELISM, ASBURY THEOLOGICAL SEMINARY

"*Holy Conversation* is fresh encouragement for the lost practice of 'talking about God in everyday life.' Richard Peace is an engaging academic thinker whose gift is to translate even this 'scary' topic into a language and experience that can be understood by all. Our churches are waiting for a book like this and the world is waiting for 'holy conversation.'"

DAVID SCHOEN, EVANGELISM MINISTER AND TEAM LEADER, LOCAL CHURCH MINISTRIES

"Richard Peace has done enormous service for the church by putting together his vast experience and storehouse of knowledge about how we can communicate Jesus Christ in the twenty-first century. As a pastor I am deeply appreciative. This will be a well-used resource by many small groups for many years to come."

PETE SCAZZERO, AUTHOR OF *THE EMOTIONALLY HEALTHY CHURCH*

"Kudos to Richard Peace for his latest book. Dr. Peace has used his extensive experience as a teacher of evangelism and practical theologian, his expertise in small group dynamics, and his commitment to the art of interpersonal communication to provide a useful study guide to help Christians and secular people talk about the gospel in ways that are comfortable, easy, and mutually beneficial and enriching."

RICHARD STOLL ARMSTRONG, ASHENFELTER PROFESSOR OF MINISTRY AND EVANGELISM EMERITUS, PRINCETON THEOLOGICAL SEMINARY

HOLY

conversation

{ TALKING ABOUT GOD
IN EVERYDAY LIFE }

Richard Peace

IVP Connect

An imprint of InterVarsity Press
Downers Grove, Illinois

InterVarsity Press
P.O. Box 1400, Downers Grove, IL 60515-1426
World Wide Web: www.ivpress.com
E-mail: email@ivpress.com

InterVarsity Press® is the book-publishing division of InterVarsity Christian Fellowship/USA®, a movement of students and faculty active on campus at hundreds of universities, colleges and schools of nursing in the United States of America, and a member movement of the International Fellowship of Evangelical Students. For information about local and regional activities, write Public Relations Dept., InterVarsity Christian Fellowship/USA, 6400 Schroeder Rd., P.O. Box 7895, Madison, WI 53707-7895, or visit the IVCF website at <www.intervarsity.org>.

Scripture quotations, unless otherwise noted, are from the New Revised Standard Version of the Bible, *copyright 1989 by the Division of Christian Education of the National Council of the Churches of Christ in the USA. Used by permission. All rights reserved.*

The article "Holy Conversations," by Richard Peace, originally appeared in the summer 2002 issue of Word & World *magazine. Used by permission.*

Design: Cindy Kiple
Images: ryasick/iStockphoto

ISBN 978-0-8308-1119-9

Printed in the United States of America ∞

Library of Congress Cataloging-in-Publication Data

Peace, Richard.
 Holy conversation: talking about God in everyday life / by Richard
Peace.
   p. cm.
 Includes bibliographical references.
 ISBN-13: 978-0-8308-1119-9 (pbk.: alk. paper)
 ISBN-10: 0-8308-1119-2 (pbk.: alk. paper)
 1. Apologetics. 2. Witness bearing (Christianity) I. Title.
 BT1103.P43 2006
 248'.5—dc22

                                                                 2006005550

P	28	27	26	25	24	23	22	21	20	19	18	17	16	15	14	13	12	11	10	9	8	7
Y	31	30	29	28	27	26	25	24	23	22	21	20	19	18	17	16	15	14	13	12	11	

CONTENTS

THE STUDY GUIDE
AT A GLANCE

1. *What's it all about?*
Learning how to talk about the gospel in natural, informal, conversational ways.

2. *Why is this important?*
Personal witness has gotten stereotyped as a confrontational monologue with a stranger when it's really meant to be an ongoing conversation with family, friends and colleagues. We need to relearn how to talk about our faith.

3. *How does this learning experience work?*
A group of five to thirteen friends meet together in a weekly small group. Each week they consider a different aspect of the gospel and how to talk about it.

4. *What happens in the small group?*
There are two sections of input each week: a story that illustrates the theme and some teaching material that amplifies the issue. And there are two sections of discussion and sharing in which the material is processed together in conversation.

5. *Is the small group the whole deal?*
No, the really important part of this learning experience is linking up with a conversation partner outside the church with whom you'll talk on a regular basis about what you are learning. This will be great fun and the best part of the whole experience—if you let it be.

6. *Beyond the group, is there any more input that will help me become a better Christian conversationalist?*
At the end of each session is a resources section that adds new input. Also each week there is a study assignment that helps deepen your grasp of the material.

7. *This sounds time consuming.*
Not really. You have the one small group session each week. It takes less than ten minutes to read the material for the session. Your discussion with your conversation partner takes place in the context of the normal conversation you have each week with him or her. And as for the study assignment and the resources material, this can take as much or as little time as you can give to it. Still, to learn a new skill takes time, but it is worth it.

8. *How long is the small group session?*
It depends. The session can be done in as little as forty-five or as long as ninety minutes.

9. *How many sessions are there in this course?*

There are twelve sessions. It's probably best to do these weekly for twelve weeks, but other formats are possible, such as doing two sessions each time you meet or doing the first six sessions at a weekend retreat, followed by six weekly sessions. Be creative in your planning.

10. *What if it is impossible to do this course with a small group?*

You can study all this on your own. Read carefully each chapter. Write out your answers to the questions in a journal. Most important of all, make sure you have a conversation partner with whom to try out what you are learning.

11. *What if I can't find a willing conversation partner who is not yet a Christian? Can I pick a conversation partner from church?*

Sure. The important thing is to have someone to talk over this material with each week. The purpose of the course is to learn how to talk with seekers about faith, so the challenge for you is to expand your circle of friends so you will have new conversation partners.

PREFACE

This project began with a magazine article. Frederick Gaiser, the editor of the Lutheran journal *Word & World* asked me to write an article that would fit into an issue he was putting together for the summer of 2002 on the theme "Conversion? Conversation?" I agreed to do so because for some time I had wanted to explore the question of what had become of the art of Christian witness. My sense was that it had been streamlined, codified and made into a three-part process consisting of (1) the story of your conversion (told in three minutes or less), (2) a plan of salvation and (3) a challenge to accept Christ then and there.

I had great doubts about what witness had become. It seemed to me that what had once been the glorious art of Christian conversation had been reduced down to a kind of telemarketing campaign for Jesus. Furthermore, our culture was no longer buying it. They were on to us. They smelled out our religious salesmanship and were having none of it.

So I wrote the article. It was published. I rather liked what I had written. In the article I called for the church to relearn the art of Christian conversation.[1] As far as I was concerned, I had done my job as an academic working in the area of practical theology. I had issued a challenge to the church about what I had come to see was a major problem that impeded the work of Christian evangelism.

The problem was that only a relatively few pastors ever read the article (I assume). What they did with it, I have no way of knowing. Certainly there was no new movement sweeping the church whereby lay Christians learned the art of holy conversation and engaged in ongoing life-changing conversations with their friends and colleagues!

I was convicted. Maybe I needed to try my hand at more than writing an academic article. Perhaps I should put together a small group study guide. (I have written and published a number of volumes of small group material.) My academic side was trumped by my ministry side. After all, I had worked for years in the ministry of evangelism prior to becoming a professor.

The opportunity to write such a manual came via the Marketplace Community. I had been consulting with Jim Luther and David Ingrassia, two very creative guys who felt God calling them to work with the business community. I helped them prepare training materials, including the

---

[1]The original article is reproduced in the appendix.

first draft of what eventually became *Holy Conversation: Talking About God in Everyday Life*. In the end the Marketplace Community failed to materialize. Jim and David went on to other productive ministries. But I had the core of this book.

I am grateful for the feedback I got on the material from small group members in the Marketplace Community, especially Jim and David, who insisted that the small group experience move from life to truth and not the other way around as was normally the case. I got useful insights from students in my Art of Evangelism class at Fuller Theological Seminary who saw an early version of this material. I had the chance to present the idea of holy conversation at the United Church of Christ (UCC) national evangelism event "God Is Still Speaking, It's All About Evangelism" in Atlanta, August 5-7, 2004. I got good feedback, especially from David Schoen, evangelism minister and team leader for the United Church of Christ.

In addition, I am grateful to the Rev. Paul Nickerson, Associate Conference Minister for Evangelism, Mission and Justice for the Massachusetts Conference of the UCC, for enabling me to try out the materials in various contexts in Massachusetts.

I have taught evangelism in the seminary context for nearly thirty years now. I continue to be amazed at how hard it is for very bright, committed seminary students to get beyond a "plan of salvation" and talk about the gospel in a conversational way. Sure, they can discuss the theological concepts that underlie the gospel, but it's often hard for them to engage in ordinary conversation about these matters using every-

day language. I don't think this is their fault. I think it is our fault in the church. We don't talk about the gospel very much in our communities. We assume that we all know what the gospel is about, that we are committed to it and that we believe in it.

Last year I was teaching an adult Sunday School class titled "What Is This Thing of Evangelism?" The context was the UCC church I belong to in Massachusetts. Evangelism has not been a central concern in our denomination until recently.[2] In one of the sessions I was explaining the idea of holy conversation, and the lights went on for one of the men in the class. "That's our problem," he said. "We just don't talk about the gospel. If we can't have this sort of conversation in church, where can we have it?" In the subsequent discussion we realized that it wasn't a lack of interest in or commitment to the gospel that impeded this kind of conversation. It just wasn't on our agenda—and we needed to get it back on the agenda.

That we need to wrestle with, reflect on, understand and process the gospel in the context of our Christian communities is newly urgent. In the past decade we have begun to learn (remember, actually) that at its heart evangelism is a community activity, not an individual process. We have begun to learn that we need to invite seekers, strangers, the interested and all others into our fellowshiping, worshiping, serving communities. Hospitality is key to evangelism. And as these folks hang out with us, join in our activities and ministries, they begin to learn the gospel. They discover in community what the church is all about, the nature of our core commit-

---

[2]The "God Is Still Speaking" campaign was launched in the UCC in 2004.

ments and what it means to follow Jesus. "Belonging before believing" is the new rubric for evangelism.

Or so the theory goes. What happens if they join us and we never really talk about our core commitments beyond the formality of the worship service? How do they "get us" if we are silent about these matters or too embarrassed to put into words what binds us together? How will they learn Christianity if we ourselves do not know how to express all this in ordinary language in the context of normal conversation?

I think the call to learn how to engage in holy conversation is no mere peripheral matter but a central challenge for the church in the twenty-first century. My hope is that this book will contribute in some way to meeting this need.

Richard Peace

INTRODUCTION

We are experiencing a fascinating moment in history. For years now religion (Christianity included) has lived on the margins of culture. People were not much interested. But all that began to change in the 1990s. Suddenly spirituality was all the rage. Interest has continued unabated ever since.

What tipped people off that something new was afoot were all those angels in 1990s. Everywhere you looked there was an angel. Take films and television, for example. In 1996 Denzel Washington played an angel in *The Preacher's Wife* (good casting). That same year John Travolta also played an angel in *Michael*. (John Travolta as an angel?) *Touched by an Angel* was a prime-time television series that was not only popular but took God seriously (though Jesus was only allowed a guest appearance in the final episodes). The majority of Americans claimed they believed in angels.

This fascination with the spiritual was everywhere: in popular music ("If God Was One of Us" by Joan Osbourne in 1995, *Supernatural*, the album of year in 2000 by Carlos Santana),[3] in books (in 1995, for the first time ever, more books were published in America on spirituality than on business), in politics (remember the recent 2004 presidential campaign?). Bookings at spiritual retreat centers blossomed. Spiritual exercises were in vogue. Everybody believed in God (well, not quite everyone, but over 95 percent according to Mr. Gallup). *In North America we are hot in the pursuit of God.*

What triggered all of this? My personal theory is that there was a conjunction of factors in the 1990s. The baby-boom generation (all 79 million of them) started into midlife. One of the characteristics of this stage of life is the so-called midlife crisis in which a person begins to ask questions about meaning, purpose, death and God. It is a spiritually introspective time. About the same time Generation X was coming into adulthood, bringing with them their flawed childhoods, loss of hope and sense of disenfranchisement. These issues created the basis for their curiosity about the spiritual.[4] But most of all, North America had moved (almost without no-

---

[3]The best thing about the album, apart from it superb musical sensibility, was the title. It was not really an exploration of spirituality. In 2002 Santana recorded an album titled *Shaman*, which goes to show that this interest in spirituality is quite broad.

[4]See Douglas Coupland's book *Life After God* (New York: Pocket Books, 1994) for a chronicle of how this played out for Gen-X.

ticing) from a modern worldview with its insistence on order and the autonomy of the individual to a postmodern world with its loss of metanarratives and openness to mystery. This was a whole new way of looking at life, and God was not excluded from the conversation.

My friend Barry Taylor tells the story of a prerelease screening he attended of the 1999 film *The Third Miracle* (starring Ed Harris and Anne Heche). Barry was the musical supervisor on the film as well as the composer of a number of the songs. (He is also a pastor.) The aim of the screening was to get feedback that would assist the producers in their postproduction work and subsequent marketing. So at the end of the screening they asked the audience about the film. But the audience didn't want to talk about the details of the film; they wanted to talk about God—the issue raised by the film. And they did so, vigorously, despite all the efforts of the producers to focus the conversation on their agenda. Here was a thoroughly secular audience pursuing its fascination with the spiritual.

So what is the point? Just this: in the forty years or so that I have been engaged in the ministry of evangelism, I have never encountered such openness to talking about the gospel. *People want to talk about God. And we need to be part of that conversation.*

TALKING ABOUT SPIRITUALITY

But we must have something to contribute to the conversation. This is the rub. Committed Christians are not always seen as good conversation partners—especially when talking about God! Why? Because we have a history of coming across with pious platitudes or canned formulas. It's like all we want to do is to convince people that we have got it right about God and that they better listen up and get with our agenda. This is *not* conversation. It's monologue. Worse than that it's ideological monologue that has little room for the give and take of ordinary conversation. We are selling a product (Jesus), not ruminating on God. We have an agenda (that they get converted), so we don't always come across as genuine or fully honest in our conversation. Nor do we really listen to others. We are too busy getting our preplanned points across.

Does this sound too harsh? Probably. Furthermore, it is a caricature of a caricature. But alas there is enough truth in this stereotype that we need to stop and consider how we understand the art of Christian witness. Are we trapped by a programmatic understanding of witness?

There is another side to the problem. So far I have been talking about people from fervent Christian traditions where witness and evangelism are central concerns. What about those of us who come from more mainline traditions where talking about our faith is not the norm? We face a different problem. It's almost as if we are slightly embarrassed about our faith, as if this isn't something to be discussed in public. So mostly we just try to do good things. We get involved in the right causes, but we seldom articulate what we believe, lest it be taken as bad manners. It's no wonder that the so-called mainline church continues its relentless decline year after year. Mainline Christians, when they think about witness, are clear about what they do *not* want to do—engage in button-hole evangelism the way the fundamentalists do. But they aren't nearly as clear about what they do want to do—except that it would be nice if more people came to church and engaged in the ministry Jesus calls us to.

All this has begun to change, however. Mainline churches are beginning to pay attention to the ministry of evangelism. The Episcopal Church declared the 1990s to be "A Decade of Evangelism." The Presbyterian Church (USA), via their "Evangelism and Witness" website offers resources for outreach, including material on the theme "Faithful Witnesses."[5] The United Church of Christ started a program called "God Is Still Speaking," which includes training in outreach as well as a national ad campaign based on a very effective video spot. In fact, eight mainline churches have teamed together to develop a new website that focuses on evangelism.[6]

A TRAINING COURSE IN HOLY CONVERSATION

Both evangelical and mainline Christians are united in a common need to learn how to talk about the Christian faith in ways that will engage positively the culture around us. This is the aim of *Holy Conversation:* to be a training program which helps meet this goal.

What I am advocating is good, red-blooded conversation about issues that

matter: conversation about God that engages each conversation partner deeply. For committed Christians to be part of such conversations we need to know how to talk about our faith. We need to be able to move beyond a carefully crafted formula into the heart of the gospel with all its mystery, wonder, hope and clarity.

So here is the proposal: the way to become this kind of conversationalist is to give serious attention to the key concepts of the gospel. We need to understand in some depth the good news of Jesus. We need to be able to talk about that good news in easy, comfortable ways without using theological jargon. We also need to experience the gospel. It is not enough just to understand—though understanding is crucial; we also need to encounter the realities to which the gospel points.

The small group. We need others in order to become this sort of conversationalist. This book is written to be a guide for a small group. Only as we talk about these things together do clarity and understanding emerge. A small group is the ideal context within which to mull over the gospel. The discussion, the musing together, the questions, the laughter and the shared insights and experiences that make up small group conversation create the perfect environment for learning a new way.

Conversation partners. But the conversation cannot stay in the small group. Holy conversation is all about engaging others beyond the circle of the church. This is why the whole concept of a "conversation

---

[5]See <www.pcusa.org./evangelism/churchdevelopment/pe-es2005.htm>, accessed on July 27, 2005.
[6]See www.evangelismconnections.org. The eight denominations are American Baptist Churches, USA; Christian Church (Disciples of Christ); Church of the Brethren; Evangelical Lutheran Church in America; Presbyterian Church (USA); Presbyterian Church in Canada; Reformed Church in America; and United Church of Christ.

partner" is central to this twelve-week series. Only as we talk through what we are learning with those not yet committed to the gospel do we understand the gospel.

This is, of course, an act of evangelism but not in the traditional sense. As you invite one or more friends to become conversation partners with you for the duration of the course, you need to be up-front and transparent about what you are asking. Your potential conversation partners need to know that you are a member of a twelve-week-long small group organized about the theme of holy conversion and that the intention of the small group is to help you learn to talk about your faith in Jesus. You need their help because your goal is to be able to be a fit conversationalist with those who do not yet follow the way of Jesus. You can't learn this art without their help. However, this is not just a disinterested exercise for you. You really believe these things (or at least are working out what you believe), and you want others to discover the reality of Jesus. You would not be the least bit sorry if out of this experiment your conversation partners became interested in Jesus. But, be that as it may, what you want from a conversation partner is someone to talk with regularly about various aspects of the gospel.

The Christian community. The small group, in turn, needs to be the reflection of a larger community: a church, a fellowship, a ministry, a house church or something similar. Conversation between friends is just the beginning. Such conversation needs to be brought into the wider arena of a Christian community. The reality of the gospel is learned, expressed and experienced in the particularity of a concrete Christian community. In the end, the Christian community is the bearer of the gospel.

The goal, of course, is that others encounter the gospel and do so in a way that brings Jesus alive for them. The hope is that they will meet Jesus and be changed. And the hope is that we will meet Jesus in a fresh way and be changed. True conversation brings about change in the lives of all the participants.

Evangelism and Conversion

Underlying involvement in a course such as this is a commitment to the ministry of evangelism. Here is yet another rub. The word *evangelism* arouses as many negative images as does the word *witnessing.* Again, it is true that some of what has been done in the name of evangelism is disreputable. Still, the word *evangelism* is a good New Testament word and describes an authentic ministry the church is (and always has been) called to.

Evangelism is problematic on several accounts. From a purely pragmatic point of view, traditional methods of evangelism no longer seem to work. Furthermore, few people seem very good at evangelism. Most of us just fumble around and get nowhere in a conversation about Christianity. Other objections to evangelism are theological. If God loves everybody, why bother?

This training manual is not the place to explore the various issues related to our motivation to do evangelism. My pragmatic answer to the question of why we do evangelism is that *Christian conversion makes a profound difference in the lives of people.*

In the end, this is what evangelism is all about: conversion to Jesus. It is about discovering who Jesus really is even as we discover who we really are. It is about deciding to stop living in destructive, unfulfilling ways and instead turn around and start following Jesus as we pursue wholeness. *Conversion* is the word we use to describe the experience of turning around and following Jesus.

How do people get converted? One step at a time—unless God gives them a mystical experience so in one moment they jump right over all of the steps to God himself (like St. Paul did). But those kinds of conversions are the exception, not the rule. Mostly it takes one step at a time, one little conversation at a time, until it all makes sense and we can say yes to Jesus from the depths of our being.

But we often imagine that all conversions are sudden, so all we have to do is to tell people what is true and they will say "Thank you very much. I want to be a Christian too." Sometimes it works this way, but mostly it takes time for people to "get it." A little bit of data here, a few musings there, an article, more conversation, conversations with other people. Slowly it all begins to make sense. And it's not just our minds that are being convinced. Something is also taking place on a deeper level. Jesus is beginning to make sense to me, to who I am in the context of where I struggle and hurt. Jesus brings my deepest aspirations alive. So I say yes to the new consciousness that has formed in me.

Christian conversion is about saying yes to Jesus, who has become for me a living person, who loves me and is willing to

forgive me at that deep spot where I most need forgiveness. I say yes to joining up with his community and his way of living. I say yes to my spiritual aspirations, moving them from the periphery of my life to the very center. The aim of holy conversation is to help people as they walk on the road to conversion.

But it isn't as if once we are converted to Jesus, our need for conversion ceases. In fact, the one conversion opens us up to a life of conversion. The "big C" conversion to Jesus points us in the right direction. The "little c" conversions of everyday life mean we continue to decide over and over again to keep walking on that path.

Conversion is good for us. We all know about notorious conversions: alcoholics snatched from the pit of their addiction to a life of sobriety, thugs who experience forgiveness and new life and go on to serve others in deep ways, nasty people who meet Jesus and become . . . well, perhaps not nice people immediately, but at least they begin to work at learning how to love others. In Brazil I heard story after story about men who beat their wives, drank away most of what they earned and mistreated their children, but who came to Jesus and literally became new people. They learned how to love their wives and families even as they worked hard and used their income to build a better life. A sort of social transformation was taking place out these conversions. Meeting God is good for us. We become better people, more of what we were intended to be and who we want to be.

So we do evangelism, quite apart from anything else, because lives get transformed when people meet Jesus. To me this is sufficient motivation for learning the art of holy conversation.

Meaningful Conversation/ Holy Conversation

So what is this thing I am calling holy conversation? Perhaps we can get at a working definition by first looking at the nature of meaningful conversation.

First, in order for meaningful conversation to flourish we need to be good conversation partners. Often Christians are not considered to be such since we seem to want to present a "plan of salvation" rather than talk things over. Meaningful conversation involves a give and take that engages both partners.

Second, meaningful conversation deals with issues of consequence. Meaningful conversation is not necessarily "heavy." It's often good fun even though the issues are "heavy" and real.

Meaningful conversation doesn't have to issue in a decision or produce a winner and a loser. Meaningful conversation is open-ended. It stops and starts and often goes on for months at a time. Meaningful conversation may produce more questions than it does answers. And it's these questions that get us thinking. Even after we say goodbye to our friend, we keep pondering what we talked about.

Meaningful conversation deepens friendship; it doesn't drive people apart. Meaningful conversation draws others into the circle of our conversation: "Hey Joe, what do you think?" It brings us into larger arenas for conversation. When we've been talking about God, it makes sense to get involved with communities where God is the center of conversation.

Meaningful conversation changes people. And the change extends to both conversation partners. One of the problems with how evangelistic conversation has gotten stereotyped is that only one person is expected to change: the other one. "As for me, well I'm the Christian. I know Jesus so I don't need to change." This is not true since each of us is on a spiritual pilgrimage in which growth and change is normal and expected. In fact, conversation produces conversion on the part of both conversation partners.

In the end, holy conversation is simply vigorous, ongoing, good-hearted conversation around the whole topic of God and how to bring God into our lives in a life-changing way. As such, it is a wonderful experience.

How to Use the *Holy Conversation* Small Group Material

Holy Conversation is a twelve-week small group training program. The aim of the program is to help laypeople become competent and confident Christian conversationalists. In the process group members will learn more about their faith. Not only will mature Christians learn how to talk about their faith, but newer Christians will deepen their understanding of core gospel truths.

This program in evangelism moves beyond the traditional gospel-outline type of presentation; engaging in holy conversation involves interaction that unfolds over time, between friends and colleagues, and touches on the key issues of the gospel. It's no longer enough to memorize an outline and then present it as a monologue. People today are fascinated by spirituality. They want to talk about God. They value your insights and experience. But they don't want dogmatic presentations. They want compassionate and honest conversation with people of faith.

So the this study provides input and experiences that seek to help Christians become comfortable in talking about key aspects of the gospel. The program is divided into three sections.

1. "Getting a Fix on the Problem" is a three-week overview that seeks to put holy conversation in the context of the spiritual pilgrimage people are on and how they hear the gospel in the midst of their search for God.

2. The heart of the program is titled "Talking About . . . ," where eight aspects of the gospel are explored, each during one small group session: Jesus, need, sin, repentance, confession, belief (in general), belief in Jesus and commitment.

3. Finally, "Putting It All Together" attempts to draw together the course in such a way that small group members are equipped and motivated to engage in holy conversation.

Small Group Structure

Each small group session consists of a series of interrelated modules of material that move from life to truth to practice. There are two input sections ("Story" and "Concept") and two discussion sections ("Life: How We Live It" and "Truth: How We Apply it").

LIFE

Story. Each small group session begins with an introduction that expresses the main idea of the session in the context of life experience. Often this takes the form of a story. The holy conversation issue is identified, as is the topic for the session.

There are several ways for the group to access the material in the story section:

- The best way is for member to read the material at home in preparation for the small group. This way saves time and allows for more conversation.

- Busy people do not always prepare, even though reading this section takes only a minute. So what you may need to do at the start of the session, after a brief introduction by the leader and prayer together, is to give the group members two minutes to read the story silently.

- You can read the story section aloud. It takes less than four minutes to do so.

- The leader can summarize the material aloud as the group follows along by scanning each paragraph.

However you do it, the key point is to get people focused on the issue and connecting to the topic.

The first section ("Life") ends with small group questions ("Life: How We Live It"). Begin the small group conversation by asking the first question and then giving each person thirty seconds or so to respond (beginning with the leader). In this way you

- get the group talking, with everyone participating

- begin to hear experiences from the life

of each person (this builds a sense of community)

- start to think together about the topic from the vantage point of life experience

Then go on to the next two questions. These are longer discussion questions, so you may not have time to discuss both questions.

Be sure to stick to the time allotted for this section (and each section). Otherwise you will not get through all the material.

TRUTH

Concept. Now we shift back to more input. This is the teaching section for the session. New material is presented. Also there is practical advice about the process of holy conversation. Sometimes there will be a case study, but at other times information will be presented. The section concludes with a summary of the main point of the session ("The Bottom Line"). Make sure the group understands the main point.

Use one of the options noted in the "Story" section to convey this input to the group.

Truth: How We Apply It. Then the focus moves back to the group, which is asked to process this material. The emphasis here is on application of the ideas. Typically there will be four discussion questions. Sometimes there is a group exercise. Try to be as practical as possible in this discussion. Keep the focus on the task of learning how to engage in holy conversation.

Take between fifteen and forty minutes for this discussion section (depending on which time schedule you are on).

PRACTICE

Study. End the session by going over the homework to be done between sessions. This is the way group members will actually become holy conversationalists.

The study section asks people to engage with the material that has been discussed.

Practice: How We Do It. This section takes practice one step further. Group members are invited to engage with their conversation partners.

End the session with prayer. You have about five minutes for this final part of the group.

RESOURCES

This section comprises additional material to read during the week related to the topic of the session.

Time and Size Parameters

Decide on how long you are able to meet each week. Obviously the more time you have the more conversation is possible. The optimum amount of time is ninety minutes per session. However, you can do a session in as little as forty-five minutes.

Total time	45 minutes	60 minutes	90 minutes
Story	5 minutes	5 minutes	5 minutes
Life: How We Live It	20 minutes	25 minutes	40 minutes
Concept	5 minutes	5 minutes	5 minutes
Truth: How We Apply It	15 minutes	25 minutes	40 minutes

Once you decide on the length of the session, be sure to stick to the times allotted to each section. Otherwise you will not get through all the material. This may mean dropping some of the questions. It will also mean limiting responses to questions.

As to the size of the small group, research indicates that groups work best when they have between five and thirteen members. When you have fewer than five members you do not have a critical mass for energetic conversation. When you have over thirteen there isn't enough time for all to participate. Perhaps the optimum number for a conversation-based group is seven. If you have more people who want to join the group, make two groups.

Number of Sessions

Holy Conversation has twelve small group sessions. It is best, of course, to do all twelve sessions. However, this is not always possible. Here are some other options if you have fewer weeks available:

Nine Weeks

1. People on a Spiritual Pilgrimage
2. Stories of the Presence of God
3. Really Good News
4. Talking About Jesus
6. Talking About Sin
8. Talking About Confession
10. Talking About Believing in Jesus
11. Talking About Commitment
12. Holy Conversation

Six Weeks

1. People on a Spiritual Pilgrimage
2. Stories of the Presence of God
3. Really Good News
4. Talking About Jesus
10. Talking About Believing in Jesus
11. Talking About Commitment

Another idea is to do two forty-five-minute sessions each week. This way you could do all twelve session in six weeks. Or you could plan a half-day retreat on a Saturday during which you do the first three sessions. The following week you would move to session four and so on.

What about the missing sessions? Add these to the homework. Invite small group members to study the missing sessions on their own.

Be creative if time is your problem.

A Message to Members of a Small Group

Small groups are great fun, and when done properly they are sources of genuine learning and real motivation. I have come to believe that we enjoy structured small groups so much because of the quality of conversation they afford us. Few other contexts in life allow us to examine topics of real interest in the company of good-hearted folk, with the anticipation of real growth and changes in our own lives.

Of course, not all small groups are created equal, and so this good experience is not always achieved. There are always reasons for the failure of a small group—but this is a topic well beyond the scope of this book. However, one factor that goes a long way in explaining groups that work is the quality of preparation on the part of individual small group members. *The more that each member of the group prepares for the session, the better the session.* It is often that simple.

This is not to say that such preparation has to be time consuming (though the more time spent, the more one has to bring to a group). It is as much a question of *attitude* as *time*. The core attitude must be: I am a key person in this small group. I have something unique to bring to it. The more I ponder the topic of a forthcoming session, the more carefully that I read the input materials, the more I think about the questions that will guide our discussion, the better able I am to be that unique point of light in the small group.

On Preparing for Each Session

- Input sections ("Story" and "Concept"). Read the two input sections for each chapter. Each can be read in just a couple of minutes—really. Pondering them will take some time, but this can be done as you go about your business during a normal day.

- In the "Story" section the core concept of the session is defined in the context of a life experience. Mull over the topic, be it faith, repentance, sin or whatever. What does the word mean to you? How do you experience this concept? How do you talk about it, if at all.

- In the "Concept" section, the core idea is worked out in more detail. The focus is on ideas: getting the concept right and getting it straight. Read this section carefully enough that you are comfort-able with the core idea and able to discuss it.

- Conversation sections ("Life: How We Live It" and "Truth: How We Apply It"). Read the questions that you will discuss. There are usually six questions, three per section, though sometimes there is an exercise.

- In "Life: How We Live It" the focus is on experience—your experience and the experience of others when it comes to the core concept of the session. You might want to think about how you would respond to each question, though sometimes the spontaneous response in the course of the group conversation is best.

- In "Truth: How We Apply It" the focus is on concepts and how to talk about them. Again think about what you might contribute to the group conversation around each question.

- Practice sections ("Study" and "Practice: How We Do It"). In the week between small group meetings there is some homework. Again, what is asked isn't time consuming, and the effort you put into this work reaps good results— for you and for the group.

- In the "Study" section you are asked to do something to deepen your grasp of the concept, be it research on the meaning of a word, reflection on your life experience or watching television to see how the idea of sin is portrayed. Not only does this deepen your understanding of the concept, but it also gives you something else to talk about with your conversation partner.

- The "Practice: How We Do It" section is all about engaging in conversation with your partner. Often there are suggestions for what you might talk about.

How long is all this going to take each week? Well, apart from the small group, which meets forty-five to ninety minutes a week, if you devote an hour per week to preparing for and responding to each session, you would learn a lot. And remember this time can be broken up into smaller chunks: ten minutes here, twenty minutes there and so on.

Engaging a Conversation Partner

What makes this small group experience different from most other small group experiences is the call to find a conversation partner who is not yet a conscious follower of Jesus. The purpose of the small group is to learn to engage in holy conversation, and this is not going to happen unless you start engaging in holy conversation!

So you need a guinea pig. Guinea pigs are used for experimentation. They help you learn. As you seek out a conversation partner, put it in these terms: you want him or her to be a guinea pig!

Be up-front and completely transparent about what you doing and why. Tell your perspective conversation partner that you are part of a church-based small group, that the purpose of the group is to learn how to talk about your faith with others and that the reason you are doing this is because the church is called to share it message with others. You might want to add that the church has not always done a

good job at this. In fact, it has a track record of being coercive, manipulative and unclear in its attempts to talk about the good news of Jesus. Your small group is all about becoming responsible Christian conversationalists.

Explain that each week the small group will consider a different topic: faith, repentance, Jesus and so forth, and how to talk about that topic with others. Tell the person that you want to try out what you are learning with him or her. Give him or her a copy of *Holy Conversation* so your partner will know what you are discussing in the small group.

It is conceivable that your friend might ask about your intentions in this exercise. "Beyond using me as a guinea pig, what do you want to see happen? Are you trying to convert me?" The answer is that, of course, you would love to see him or her converted to Christ, and this would be a wonderful outcome of your ongoing conversation. However, that is not up to you. It is up to God. All you really want is faith-oriented conversation.

You have nothing to hide, and the more candid you can be the better.

Pick someone you see in the normal course of everyday life. This works a lot better when you see your conversation partner on a regular basis. Then you can talk in bits and pieces over the course of a week. Still, it also works if you have, say, a weekly breakfast with a friend. Holy conversation is best face to face, but a weekly phone conversation might have to suffice. I suppose an ongoing e-mail conversation could work, but that is not voice-to-voice communication and is less than a true conversation in that it can't invoke the whole human sensorium of sound, sight, touch and body language that goes into a good conversation.

Each week you get to talk about your experience with your conversation partner. In the so-called seventh question (the final question in each session which is usually, but not always, question 7), you are asked to reflect in various ways on your ongoing conversation.

GETTING A FIX ON THE PROBLEM

1

PEOPLE ON A
SPIRITUAL PILGRIMAGE

life

Everybody is on a spiritual pilgrimage. Everybody. Even the guy who curses God. True, he may be going in the wrong direction (away from God), but he's still on a spiritual journey. He can't help it. This is the way God made us—with a nature that is meant to be in touch with the supernatural.

We are creatures designed to inhabit two worlds: the natural and the spiritual. Lots of writers have commented on the fact that there is an inner restlessness until we pay attention to our spiritual side.

And lots of people are paying attention to their spiritual side these days—which is good news. The bad news is that they seem to lack any sense of where they are situated in their spiritual pilgrimage or how to move forward in a Godward direction.

Tim grew up in a religious home but was having none of it. He rebelled in high school. He rebelled in college. He made an art out of rebelling against the worldview of his Christian parents. If asked, he would say that he was an *agnostic* when it came to the God issue. He was not quite willing to say there was no God. That took too much faith. (Atheists have to have lots of faith.) On the other hand, Tim certainly couldn't find sufficient evidence to believe in God.

Cary, on the other hand, does believe in God, but her God is more akin to a cosmic force than anything personal. To her, prayer is the means whereby we tap into this spiritual force for our own good and the good of the planet. Though she doesn't know it, she is what might be called a *deist*. Clearly she is at a different point in the spiritual pilgrimage than Tim.

Wendy is a *seeker*. She knows God is personal. For her the question is how to connect with this God. Leigh, on the other hand, is *disillusioned*. Once an enthusiastic Christian, she was seduced by

STORY:
*Spiritual
Pilgrims*
(5 minutes)

the associate pastor of her church and then accused of being a "temptress" by the elders in the church (who allowed the pastor in question to keep his job). She is stalled out in her spiritual pilgrimage, unable to get over the hurt she experienced at the hands of church leaders. Martin is *contented* with his life. He has a great job, a beautiful wife, cute kids and a nice house. God is not needed. Martin already has it all. Susan knows she needs God. The problem is that to follow God means she has to give up her *hedonistic* lifestyle, and she likes sex and all those cocktails far too much to do that.

Agnostics, atheists, deists, seekers, the disillusioned, the contented, the hedonists—lots of names for different stopping places on the spiritual pilgrimage.

The point is that different people are at different places in their spiritual pilgrimages. *Our conversation needs to focus on the particular issues that engage each person when it comes to God.* So in this session we will explore the shape of spiritual pilgrimage.

LIFE:
How We
Live It
(20, 25 or 40
minutes)

1. What was your pilgrimage to God like? Consider the phases you went through in your pilgrimage of faith. What helped you move toward God?

2. Do you know people who fit the spiritual profile of any of those mentioned above?

3. Think about the people you know and give a name (your best guess) to where each person might be at in his or her spiritual pilgrimage.

truth

The whole idea of spiritual pilgrimage is articulated most clearly in Hebrews 11—12, but the concept itself is embedded deep within the Judeo-Christian tradition. The people of Israel were a pilgrim people beginning with Abraham and Sarah, who literally trekked all over the Middle East as God brought them into the Promised Land. In the New Testament the pilgrimage was more an inner journey than an actual journey. Mark tells the story of the spiritual pilgrimage of the twelve apostles. In Acts we read about the faith journey of the Ethiopian eunuch, of Saul who became Paul the apostle, and even of Peter whose journey didn't stop with his commitment to Jesus but continued with his new openness to Gentiles.

CONCEPT: *The Idea of Pilgrimage*

(5 minutes)

The concept of *spiritual journey* is a useful one when it comes to evangelism. For one thing, this understanding helps us to realize that *every person we meet is on a spiritual journey.* No one is the enemy. Each is a beloved prodigal who needs to be called back to his or her real home with God.

Second, we realize that *we too are on a spiritual pilgrimage.* We are at a different place than the seekers we talk to, but we are just as answerable to God as the agnostic who is not sure God exists. Each of us is answerable to God; each is called to move forward in our pilgrimage. This understanding gets rid of the us-them mentality that has spoiled some evangelism in the past. ("You sinners have the problem. We righteous have the answers, so listen carefully to what we have to say.") Now it is both of us seeking the way forward.

Third, we realize that different people are at different places with the result that *each person has his or her own issues to deal with* before he or she can get to the question of Jesus. For some it is proof or plausibility that God exists. For others, the question has to do with the demands of the gospel. For still others, the issue is whether God is a force or a person. Some have to wrestle with what went wrong with their prior religious experience, while others have to try to match up their views of spirituality with what Scripture teaches us about God and how to meet Jesus. So holy conversation takes place around these personal issues.

I have come to think about the spiritual journey as having three parts: (1) quest (in which we explore the question of God),

(2) commitment (in which we move through various stages until we commit ourselves to Jesus as his disciples), and (3) formation (in which we grow in our faith over time).[1]

Our task, therefore, is to relate to others as men and women who are on a spiritual journey (even if they are not yet aware of it), knowing that we are on that same journey (though probably at a different point). Holy conversation involves sharing with one another the complexities and challenges of that journey with the aim of gaining clarity into where we are in the journey and what questions we need to deal with in order to take the next step forward in that journey.

The bottom line. The task of evangelism is to help others come to the place in their spiritual pilgrimage so that they are able to hear Jesus' call to become his disciples. However, people often need to wrestle with a variety of questions and challenges before they reach this point. Our call is to walk with them on their journey of faith even as we share with them our own ongoing journey of faith.

TRUTH:
How We
Apply It
(15, 25 or 40 minutes)

1. What difference does it make in your relationship to others when you consider them to be men and women on a spiritual journey rather than viewing them as hostile to faith, disinterested in God or deluded about spiritual matters?

2. What resources, events, gatherings or experiences might help those you know to become active and engaged spiritual pilgrims?

3. What kind of conversation might you have with a Tim, Cary, Wendy, Leigh, Martin or Susan?

4. How is your search going for a conversation partner?

---

[1]See "The Geography of Pilgrimage" in my book *Conversion in the New Testament* (Grand Rapids: Eerdmans, 1999), pp. 311-18.

practice

Work on refining your understanding of the shape of your own spiritual pilgrimage. What was your childhood faith like? Adolescent faith? Adult faith? What was your quest phase like? your committed phase? formation phase? How did you move forward in your pilgrimage? Was there also backward movement? What significant events raised spiritual questions for you? Who were the people along the way who helped you in your faith pilgrimage?

STUDY

The clearer you are about your spiritual pilgrimage, the easier it will be for you to talk about this with others.

Talk over this whole idea of spiritual pilgrimage with your conversation partner. Share your thinking about your own pilgrimage. Get your partner to talk about his or her religious pilgrimage. Bring no agenda to this conversation. Just be open, honest and curious.

PRACTICE:
How We Do It

resources

Quest is the first phase of a spiritual pilgrimage. People wrestle with the question of God and their relationship to God. It is helpful to know the names of various stopping points in the spiritual quest. By knowing where a person is at in his or her spiritual pilgrimage you are better able to enter into useful conversation. Each person has a key question to face which, when answered, leads to growth in a Godward direction.

The Spiritual Quest: Stopping Places and Challenging Questions

What follows is a representative list of positions, not a complete list of all the stopping places in the quest phase. These stopping places are in no particular order. In real life, people's positions are more complex than the list below might suggest. And the questions faced at each position are also representative. Actual issues are often more complex and less focused. Still, by having some sort of typology of pilgrimage it helps us in our conversation.

- *Agnostic* (someone who is not sure whether there is a God or not). Key question: How can I know if there is a God?

- *Atheist* (someone who does not believe God exists). Key question: Is there a God?

- *Deist* (someone who believes God is an impersonal force). Key question: Is God personal?

- *Intellectual believer* (someone who believes in God but who is not committed to God). Key question: What does God demand of me?

- *Seeker* (someone who wants to know God). Key question: How can I know God?

- *Indifferent* (someone who has ceased caring about the issue of God). Key question: What is the meaning of life?

- *Given over to evil* (someone who has chosen to follow God's enemy). Key question: What price am I paying?

- *Contented* (someone who has it all and doesn't need God). Key question: How do I deal with disaster?

- *Disillusioned* (someone who once believed but has lost faith). Key question: What went wrong with my religious experience?

- *Alternate faith* (someone who follows another religious tradition). Key question: Am I in a vital relationship with God?

- *Hedonist* (someone whose god is pleasure). Key question: What price do I pay for my pleasure?

- *Relativist* (someone who believes it doesn't matter what you believe). Key question: How do I deal with such a thing as the Holocaust?

2

STORIES OF THE PRESENCE OF GOD

Everybody loves a good story. Witness how much time we spend each week watching the endless dramas available to us on television. At family gatherings we tell stories to one another. As we gather around the water cooler, mostly what we do is tell stories. It may be the story of how the New England Patriots were able to beat Payton Manning and the Indianapolis Colts in order to go the Super Bowl. Or it may be about the latest "unbelievably cute" thing your granddaughter said. Or it may be a rehash of the latest episode of the *Simpsons,* but it is a story. We love stories.

It was a story that made faith come alive for Jessica. Her friend Carol had talked a lot about Jesus, and while Jessica was interested it never connected with her—at least not until Carol told her story about healing. It seems that Carol had been ill with the flu for quite some time. It just would not go away. She would start to feel better and return to work, and two days later she would be back home in bed. Her doctor gave her various pills, but nothing helped—until one day when a friend visited Carol. Seeing how weary and weak Carol had become, her friend asked if she might pray for her. She said that sometimes when she laid hands on a person and prayed, healing happened. And that is just what happened for Carol. Two days later she was back at work, weak but okay. And the flu symptoms never returned.

What impressed Jessica was not so much that Carol was healed but the way Carol told the story. Carol really believed God healed her. She didn't make a big deal about it. Mostly what she expressed was gratitude to God. It was all so real. Jessica got to thinking. Maybe there is a God who is active in this world.

We all have stories to tell about our experience of God—stories

STORY:
God in Daily Life
(5 minutes)

that reveal the aliveness of God. And this is the place to begin when it comes to holy conversation. We share our various stories about our interaction with God—and about God's interaction with us. These don't have to be big stories. The small, ordinary ones are often best. But they need to be real. God is alive and active in life, and we can and do experience that fact. This is an important part of holy conversation.

LIFE:
*How We
Live It*
(20, 25 or 40
minutes)

1. Tell a brief story about when God first came alive for you.

2. How do stories help us in our quest to make sense out of life?

3. What stories have you heard that helped you know that God is alive and active in our lives?

truth

CONCEPT:
*Discovering
and Telling
Our Stories
of God*
(5 minutes)

Holy Conversation often begins with our stories about God: how we experienced God, how we were changed by God, how God met us in our need. Our stories say to others that God isn't just a distant idea. God is an immediate presence. As we tell stories from our spiritual pilgrimage, others start thinking about their experiences of God.

The one personal story that many Christians have learned to tell is the story of their conversion. That can be powerful, but it's only one story. We need to have available multiple personal stories of the aliveness of God which we can draw on to pepper our conversation.

So begin to reflect on your experience of God. Was God alive for you as a child? What answers to prayer do you remember most vividly? What are the most dramatic experiences you have had of God? What is the character of your daily experience with God? Is God alive for you in church and in your fellowship? Where do you meet God?

These don't have to be dramatic stories. Sometimes the quiet, ordinary stories are the most powerful. Nor do these stories have to be about success and accomplishment, like how God enabled you to win the marathon or get the contract. Stories about how God met us in failure ring true and allow others to reach out to God in their need.

But don't forget the dramatic stories. When was God's presence made known to you in a mystical experience (be it overwhelming or gentle)? When did you first sense the presence of God in your life? How did you encounter God in nature? In the stillness? At a holy place? In a dream? In music or art?

Tell the ordinary stories about how you grudgingly chose the good when you really wanted to be selfish or wicked. Tell about little answers to prayer, like when you needed special strength to get through a hard meeting and God gave you that. But also talk about the big answers, like when you needed an apartment and despite all your efforts you could find nothing. Then it came down to the last day and in your fear and anxiety you cried out to God, and the phone rang a few minutes later with just the right place for you. Don't worry about proving this was really an answer from God and not just coincidence. Just share your experience.

When did God rescue you from harm or from your own foolishness? How has God changed you? There is no need to overclaim transformation. We are all "works in progress." But those little steps toward wholeness are important.

How have you experienced love, joy, peace, longsuffering or any of the other gifts of the Holy Spirit? What about unusual gifts like healing or flashes of wisdom? What gifts has the Holy Spirit given you, and how have you used these?

Collect stories—yours and those of others (but give credit where credit is due). Become a storyteller. This is what brings holy conversation alive.

Remember the characteristics of a good story. It has a *beginning* that grabs your attention because it connects with you, is funny or is unusual. Then a good story has a solid *middle* in which you sketch the details of the event. Remember it is details that bring stories alive. The *ending* of the story is key. Draw it all together. If the ending is unexpected, all the better. Listen to good storytellers (like Garrison Keillor on his radio show *The Prairie Home Companion*) and learn from them. Work at bringing your own experiences to life.

Be honest in your stories, especially when talking about your experiences of God. Tell it like it is. Resist the temptation to embellish. Resist the temptation to make it all come out neat or right. Make sure your stories have the ring of reality because they are honest and true.

The stories can be long, but often the best stories for use in conversation are short and to the point.[1]

The bottom line. In order to engage in holy conversation we need to learn to tell our own stories of God. We need to recall various incidents, both big and small, in which we experienced the aliveness of God. Then we need to craft these into good stories that will fit into our ordinary conversation.

TRUTH:
How We
Apply It
(15, 25 or 40 minutes)

1. Identify five or six experiences in the past and present in which God was alive for you.

2. Recount in detail one of these stories.

3. Critique each other's stories as stories. What works for you? How could they be better told?

4. Discuss together your experience in finding a conversation partner and what you are learning out of this experience.

---

[1]See my two books in the 1998 Spiritual Formation Series by NavPress that will help you remember stories of God's interaction in your life: *Spiritual Journaling: Recording Your Journey Toward God* and *Spiritual Autobiography: Discovering and Sharing Your Spiritual Story.*

practice

Make a list of as many experiences as you can remember that showed the aliveness of God and the reality of Jesus. Use the categories above to jog your memory. Once you have identified a dozen or so stories, try telling them aloud to yourself.

STUDY

Now tell these stories to others, especially your conversation partner. Remember that the most effective stories are those that fit into the flow of the conversation.

PRACTICE:
How We Do It

resources

Don't be limited to your own stories about God. Collect stories from other people.

There Are Lots of Good Stories Out There

The best way to do this is to ask friends, family, colleagues and neighbors to tell you their stories. Ask them about God—not so much about what they think about God as about the experiences of God they might have had.

You will be amazed at what you hear. Everybody has a spiritual autobiography, even those who wonder about the existence of God. Now they may call these experiences by other names: "anomalies," "curious things I've experienced," "touches of grace," "odd events," "strange coincidences" and so on. Everybody has had abnormal experiences. One national study discovered that one-third of adult Americans have had what can best be described as mystical experiences, though most of these people seldom have talked about these experiences (even while considering them to be among the most important things ever to have happened to them).

And don't worry about trying to interpret these stories for others: "Oh that was God you were experiencing." Just let the stories be. Instead, tell some of your own stories. This is a great way to engage in holy conversation. Out of this sort of sharing will come the sense that God is out there (or in us) somewhere, and we need to start noticing.

For example, get people talking about death. Grace often clusters around the trauma of death. People have remarkable experiences of comfort in the time of trial, the experience of unexpected strength, dreams that seem to assure them that the beloved one is safe after death and so on. When you start sharing such stories you quickly get to the idea of the supernatural.

God stories are so powerful that many people have written about their experiences. Read these books. A good place to start is with Hugh Kerr and John Mulder's book titled *Famous Conversions: The Christian Experience* (Eerdmans, 1983). This is a collection of stories from people down through the centuries, from St. Augustine to Charles Colson. What will surprise you is the great variety in conversion stories. Apparently, God cannot be put in a box. God meets humans in all sorts of ways. Or pick up a book such as *Traveling Mercies* by Anne Lamott (Anchor, 2000). Not only is her story amazing—God just kept pursuing her through thick and thin—but Lamott is also a first-rate writer (and very funny). Another recent story is by Donald Miller, called *Blue Like Jazz* (Thomas Nelson, 2003); Miller is the quintessential postmodern Gen-Xer. Don't forget the old guys either, like C. S. Lewis *(Surprised by Joy)* or Thomas Merton *(The Seven Storey Mountain)*. Mother Teresa *(Mother Teresa: In My Own Words)* and the other Teresa (of Ávila) are worth reading as well *(The Life of Saint Teresa of Ávila by Herself)*. Kathleen Norris describes her experiences in a Benedictine monastery in *The Cloister Walk* (Riverhead, 1997). There really are a lot of good books like these out there, so collect stories from them. (Be sure to credit the stories properly, of course!)

Perhaps the best story of all is your own story. You might find my book *Spiritual Autobiography: Discovering and Sharing Your Spiritual Story* (NavPress, 1998) a useful guide to writing this particular story.

3
REALLY GOOD NEWS

life

Seth sat down next to a guy on the bus. The bus ride was long. They got talking. The guy was an enthusiastic Christian. Seth liked him. He liked his energy and his obvious passion for God. When they parted his conversation partner left Seth with a tract titled "The ABCs of the Gospel." Ordinarily Seth would have tossed away such a thing. But the guy had some interesting things to say. So Seth read the tract.

At least he tried to read it. With the best will in the world he just didn't get it. It was like the tract was written in a foreign language. He knew the words, but he didn't get how they fit together. Although he had not been raised in the church, Seth knew a little Christian vocabulary so he had some idea what "salvation" was all about. He knew words like *faith* and *Jesus*. But other words threw him. He didn't know what *repent* means, much less what it means to "invite Jesus into your heart." In the end Seth tossed the tract in the wastebasket. He was a little sorry. The guy on the bus had obviously found something. Seth wished he knew what it was.

Sound familiar? There once was a time in this culture when everybody knew the stories from the Bible and understood the core ideas of Christianity. They might not have liked these ideas, believed the stories or understand what it all meant, but at least they had heard about all this. Christianity was part of the common cultural currency. However, from the baby-boom generation on, Christian stories and ideas have dropped out of circulation in the wider culture.

So when we talk about the gospel, we need to do so in words that compute for other people. This is a key communication principle: in the end *it doesn't matter what you say; it only matters what is heard.* Communication is about what gets transmitted to other people. We talk about the gospel a lot in this country. But for the most part it is

STORY:
Telling the Story
(5 minutes)

not really understood. Or even worse, it's misunderstood; people end up with the wrong ideas about the gospel.

Guess whose responsibility it is to translate theological words into common words? Not the person hearing them! This is our job. Theological translation is about understanding gospel words at such a depth that we can talk about them in common words and ordinary images. This ability is at the very heart of holy conversation.

It's not enough just to tell our stories about God. We need to learn to tell God's story of Jesus. Witness has both a subjective side (our story) and an objective side (the story of Jesus). Often we find it relatively easy to tell our stories. The challenge is to learn to tell the gospel story with power, conviction, clarity and compassion.

LIFE:
How We
Live It

(20, 25 or 40
minutes)

1. Share an experience in which you tried to talk about your faith. How did it go? What were the good parts? The not so good parts?

2. What do your nonchurch friends think the following words mean?

   • Salvation

   • Jesus

   • Repentance

   • Faith

   • Sin

   • Hell

   • Grace

3. How well do you do at talking about Christianity in nontheological words?

truth

What exactly is the gospel? We know the answer to this question in rough terms. The gospel is about salvation. It's about trusting Jesus. It's about Jesus dying for our sins. But most of us would be hard-pressed to summarize the gospel in a few sentences—even if we were allowed to use untranslated theological words.

I have an exercise I sometimes do with my theological students. I ask them to imagine what they would say to a friend they met at a reunion who, upon hearing that they are in seminary, asks: "What is this gospel you Christians are always talking about?" I try to make it easy for the students. I ask them merely to identify the various theological words that make up the gospel. Usually they come up with a list of twenty to twenty-five words, some of which are very esoteric like *propitiation* and *regeneration.*

✳ Paul defines the gospel for us in 1 Corinthians 15:1-8:

> Now I would remind you, brothers and sisters, of the good news that I proclaimed to you, which you in turn received, in which also you stand, through which also you are being saved, if you hold firmly to the message that I proclaimed to you—unless you have come to believe in vain.
>
> For I handed on to you as of first importance what I in turn had received: that Christ died for our sins in accordance with the scriptures, and that he was buried, and that he was raised on the third day in accordance with the scriptures, and that he appeared to Cephas, then to the twelve. Then he appeared to more than five hundred brothers and sisters at one time, most of whom are still alive, though some have died. Then he appeared to James, then to all the apostles. Last of all, as to one untimely born, he appeared also to me.

Notice that Paul's focus is on Jesus, that Paul recites historical events that took place at the end of Jesus' life (Jesus died, he was buried, he rose, he appeared), and that Paul gives two words of interpretation (that this happened "according to the Scriptures" and that Jesus died "for our sins"). The gospel is all about Jesus and his death and resurrection. The mention of "our sins" shifts the focus from Jesus to the human predicament Jesus dealt with. The gospel is about dealing with human need, failure and transgression (sin).

CONCEPT:
Defining the
Gospel

(5 minutes)

Add to this what Jesus himself says about the gospel as reported in Mark 1:14-15:

> Now after John was arrested, Jesus came to Galilee, proclaiming the good news of God, and saying, "The time is fulfilled, and the kingdom of God has come near; repent, and believe in the good news."

Our response to the work of Jesus on our behalf is repentance and faith (belief).

Our focus in this session is on the gospel in overview. In the weeks ahead we will look carefully at each of these core aspects of the gospel. Our aim is theological translation: the ability to talk about these concepts in everyday language so that they make sense to others.

The bottom line. Holy conversion revolves around the gospel, so it is crucial that we have a good understanding of its content and that we can talk about it in nontheological terms. The central focus of the gospel is Jesus. We need to learn to talk about him (our subject in chap. 4). The death of Jesus deals with the problem of sin (our focus in chaps. 5-6). We respond to Jesus via repentance and faith (chaps. 7-10). The outcome is commitment to Jesus (chap. 11).

TRUTH:
How We
Apply It
(15, 25 or 40 minutes)

Analyze the tract titled "The ABCs of the Gospel."

1. Go through the tract and circle every word or phrase that might not have been understood or might have been misunderstood by Seth.

2. Discuss together the circled words and think about how you could talk about these concepts using ordinary words.

3. How is your discussion with your conversation partner going?

Are you saved? The Bible says that all men are lost. See Rom 3:23 and 6:23. This means you are lost; and lost men need to be saved.

Here is how to become a Christian. It's as simple as ABC.

A—Admit You Are a Sinner.

- Admit your need—that you are a lost sinner in need of God's grace.
- Admit the evil of your ways.
- Admit that your righteousness is like filthy rags (Is 64:6).

B—Believe on the Lord Jesus Christ.

- Believe that Christ died for your sins on the Cross (Rom 5:8).
- Believe that Jesus bore your very transgressions to Calvary and there shed His blood to secure your redemption.
- Believe that by His resurrection you are justified.
- Believe that by faith in Jesus' atoning death you will be forgiven and regenerated.

C—Confess Jesus.

- Confess your willingness to repent.
- Confess your faith by prayer and commit yourself to Jesus.
- Invite Him into your heart as your Lord and Master.
- Receive Him as your personal Savior.
- Confess Him before others.

Lost men can be saved!
This is the glorious Gospel news!
Admit, Believe and Confess and you too will be saved.

The ABCs of the Gospel

Pick one of the misunderstood words in "The ABCs of the Gospel." Do some research on it. Consult a Bible dictionary to make sure you really understand the word. Think about ways to communicate that word in nontheological terms. Is there a metaphor, image or story that might communicate this concept?

STUDY

PRACTICE:
How We Do It

Try out this word in your normal conversation. Talk to your conversation partner about the research you are doing into the meaning of this word. Get his or her insights. Discuss experiences your conversation partner might have had of people witnessing to him or her about the gospel. How was the experience?

resources

The Content of the Gospel

Objective witness. Sometimes when we share our faith we focus solely on our personal experience of Jesus. While it is important to talk about experience, it's also necessary to talk about who it is we experience. There are three major facts of the gospel that need to be touched upon:

1. Jesus (who he is and what he has done)

   - *Who Jesus is.* This will get us into a discussion about how Jesus is perceived in culture (as a great teacher, a prophet, a religious leader, etc.), about who Jesus claimed to be (the Messiah, who is the Son of God), and about Jesus' claims about himself and how to assess these.

   - *What Jesus has done.* We need to discuss the death and resurrection of Jesus. The death of Jesus makes it possible for men and women to know God. The resurrection of Jesus demonstrates the validity of his claims about himself and signifies that he is still alive and thus able to enter into relationship with us. Be prepared to discuss the historical evidence for Jesus' resurrection. See John Stott's book *Basic Christianity* for a lucid and useful discussion of the facts of Jesus.[1]

2. People (who we are from God's perspective and the nature of our plight)

   - *Human nature.* From God's perspective, humanity is in rebellion against God: wayward, lost, disobedience and willful. This

---

[1]However, it also needs to be said that historical evidence of this sort does not carry a lot of weight with postmodern people who distrust our ability to discern such matters. Still, knowing that there is a solid case for the resurrection helps people understand that the resurrection is plausible if not provable (in terms of their presuppositions about historical fact). This subject will be touched on in chapter nine.

saddens God; his children whom he loves are living in "the far country" as prodigals, unaware that their loving parent is calling them home where a joyous party awaits them.

- *Human need.* We experience our "lostness" in various ways: as a lack of purpose; as moral failure, through broken relationships; by means of depression, rage and fear; by "hitting bottom"; in the experience of hard times; and so forth. It's important to remember when we are discussing these matters that we can't convince (much less convict) other people of their need to know God (that is the work of the Holy Spirit). But we can name for them the root cause of their experiential distress. And we can model openness about our own experience of lostness. As we are open about who we really are, others are given the freedom to be open about who they are. Appropriate transparency is a key ingredient of friendship.

3. Commitment (how needy people can meet Jesus)

    - *Repentance.* This is a word that signifies our willingness to stop running away from God and to return home. It is the mental decision to turn around and go back to God.

    - *Faith.* Faith is the kind of trust that reaches out to God, believing that by the death and resurrection of Jesus we are forgiven and can have new life. Faith focuses on Jesus.

    - *Discipleship.* When we turn to Jesus we start a new life in which we seek to live as Jesus lives. This involves a revolution in how we think, what we feel, how we behave and what we give ourselves to. Conversion is the first step in what will be a whole life of following Jesus.

Subjective witness. It is not enough simply to discuss the facts. We need to share how we have been changed by those facts. We need to talk about our experience of Jesus. To do this we need

- A *vocabulary* that communicates to ordinary people. We need to translate the language of Scripture into the words, images, metaphors and stories that connect with those who have no church background.

- An *awareness* of God's presence in our lives. God is always active in us. The problem is that we don't always notice. God is present in nature around us, in the events of the day, in our needs and longings, and when we consciously reach out to God via Scripture reading, prayer and worship. We need to develop the kind of consciousness that notices the footprints of God through our lives.

- A *willingness* to talk about God. Christian witness is not learning an outline and dumping it on others via a monologue. Christian witness is not sharing the few momentous experiences we have had of God (like our conversion). Rather, Christian witness is simply being honest in our lives and our conversations about our ongoing experience of God. Mostly what we talk about with others are the little events in life (like an insight, an answer to prayer, a sense of joy, an experience of fellowship). Sometimes we share major events (like healings, mystical experiences).

Holistic witness is both subjective and objective, given in a spirit of love and openness, part of a real conversation (as opposed to a canned presentation), based on genuine listening to the others, with the assumption that we are all God's children, even those who have yet to acknowledge this fact.

Print witness. There is a longstanding tradition in the church of printing tracts. Christian tracts are short essays (for the most part) dealing with various aspects of the gospel. Mostly they are used as a means of witness. The idea is that you may not be able to express the gospel well, but this tract does it for you. So if you give it to a friend, she or he might get converted.

The problem is that tracts have a spotty history. Sure, modern tracts are often clever, even witty, and they use good graphics. But most of them operate out of an us-versus-them mentality. Recipients are addressed as if they are the enemy, spiritually clueless and damned to hell. That doesn't make for very receptive readers! Besides, the tracts are often heavy on theological language. They may read well to an insider, but for a person outside the church they are from another planet.

It's not that I am against print witness. I have written and published tracts (of a sort). One of my "tracts" was turned into a bookmark and used in a countrywide Bible distribution campaign on college campuses. Still, I do wonder if tracts are not a thing of the past? You don't see tractlike materials used in any other areas of life these days.

And by the way, I wrote "The ABCs of the Gospel." I have never published it (except here), nor would I ever use it because it is so hard to understand. But it is similar in language and style to many actual tracts that I have seen. And it makes a point: we need to clean up our theological language if we want to communicate.

An argument could be made that while the language and style of "The ABCs of the Gospel" is hopeless, the theology behind it is not so off base. It does not capture what one might call "the whole gospel," but behind the archaic words and phrases there is a living, resurrected Savior who longs to meet us. So while "The ABCs of the Gospel" does not communicate well to those who are unfamiliar with biblical language, it does state many of the central truths of the gospel. It serves as a living reminder that we need to learn the art of theological translation.

TALKING ABOUT . . .

4

TALKING ABOUT JESUS

Jesus is at the very center of the gospel. The good news is all about Jesus—who he is and what he has done for the human race. In the end, it is all about Jesus. Therefore, *Jesus is the focal point of holy conversation*. So the first order of business is to learn how to talk about Jesus.

One the one hand this is easy. Most people in North America know about Jesus. With all those Christmas pageants and Easter celebrations, Jesus is no stranger. But, on the other hand, knowledge about Jesus is pretty minimal.

Mark had heard about Jesus from the time he was a kid. He had been to church on occasion. But if asked about Jesus, Mark was likely to tell you that Jesus was a great religious teacher—although he himself didn't know much about what Jesus actually taught. Something about love, he thought. Mark knew that Jesus was a prophet who got in trouble with the law and got himself killed on a cross, which was how they did it in those days. And the rumor was that Jesus rose from the dead, though Mark was not sure about that.

Perhaps our chief challenge in holy conversation is learning how to talk about Jesus in a way that moves beyond the shallow stereotypes and limited information people have about him. How can we help people see the wonder of Jesus? That he was God become human. Fully divine yet fully human.

Fortunately we have a rich source of stories about Jesus in the Gospel accounts in the New Testament, which show who Jesus is. We just have to learn how to tell these stories in fresh and accurate ways so that in our conversation we can say, "Well, there is this story about Jesus when he met up with . . ." and off we go into a paraphrase of one of the Gospel stories.

We need to tell stories about the birth of Jesus, about how he

STORY:
*Telling the
Story of Jesus*
(5 minutes)

gathered disciples and began his ministry, about how the crowds flocked to him while the religious leaders shunned him. We need to tell stories about Jesus as a teacher, a healer and an exorcist. (No need to avoid the stories that might raise the eyebrows of people.) We need to talk about his wonderful interaction with all sorts of people, from religious leaders to fishermen and farmers to children and the marginalized. We especially need to tell the story of Jesus' death and resurrection, and what all that means.

So the first challenge when it comes to holy conversation is to learn to tell stories about Jesus. We have read the stories in the Gospels. Now we have to learn how to tell them in fresh ways, appropriate to the flow of the conversation.

LIFE:
How We
Live It

(20, 25 or 40 minutes)

1. What is one story about Jesus that has had an impact on you? Tell it in your own words and explain its impact.

2. How would your friends respond if you asked them, "Who is Jesus?" What would they get right? What would they get wrong?

3. What story about Jesus is apt to catch their attention? Why? In what context would the telling of this story be appropriate?

truth

I was amazed at how Dean could capture the attention of thirty-five loud, laughing, fun-loving teenagers at a Young Life meeting. Even more amazing, he kept their attention for the next fifteen to twenty minutes while "preaching" to them. Of course, it wasn't like an ordinary sermon. Dean's talk was fast paced and filled with stories. The kids loved the stories—even the stories about Jesus, especially when they were told in fresh ways. They also liked the illustrations, the more bizarre the better. *Stories.* That is the key to success for Young Life leaders.

This is the key to success for us too when we talk about Jesus. We just need to tell stories about Jesus. The challenge, however, is to learn how to tell these stories in an engaging way. We are used to reading stories about Jesus, but that doesn't really work in a conversation.

How do we do this? Basically we just need to *paraphrase* Gospel stories. By this I mean we need to tell the story in our own words. Good stories have a lot of detail, so we need to know about what life was like in first-century Israel. A good story has an intriguing beginning that catches people's attention. A good story moves from point to point—quickly. A good story has an appropriate ending— one that is unexpected or proves a point. A good story fits the context in which we tell it.

This means we need to understand the Jesus stories well enough to put them in our own words. We need to learn to tell a few good stories about Jesus. We need to practice telling these stories to one another.

But what stories? Well, start with your favorites—like his encounter with Nicodemus (John 3:1-21) or the rich young ruler (Mark 10:17-30) or the woman at the well (John 4:1-42). You don't have to tell the whole story. This is not Bible study. And you might want to add background to the story that will make it come alive. (Just make sure your background is accurate!)

Or you could use the six sections of Mark's Gospel (which was the first written Gospel) to organize your thinking. Pick one story from each section. Remember Mark is trying to help his readers understand who Jesus is by illuminating one key title in each section.

CONCEPT:
How to Tell Stories
(5 minutes)

- *Jesus as a great teacher.* This is a good place to start since most people consider Jesus to be a great teacher. You could use the story of his healing of the man with leprosy (Mark 1:40-45). Remember that first-century rabbis did three things: they taught, they healed and they cast out demons.

- *Jesus as a powerful prophet.* Tell the story of the healing of the demon-possessed man (Mark 5:1-20).

- *Jesus as the Messiah.* You need to tell the story of Peter's confession at Caesarea Philippi (Mark 8:27-33).

- *Jesus as the Son of Man.*[1] In Mark 10:32-45 Jesus defines the role of the Son of Man.

- *Jesus as the Son of David.* The clearing of the Temple is a great story (Mark 11:15-19).

- *Jesus as the Son of God.* The death of Jesus reveals who he is (Mark 15:33-39).[2]

Remember your goal in all this is to tell stories about Jesus that reveal who Jesus is in all his wonder, power and glory. Your stories are no substitute for the original stories in the New Testament. Hopefully your listeners will get so interested that they will want to read the stories for themselves. Even better, they might accept your invitation to join a Bible study in which you explore together one of the Gospels. Or they might come to church with you and hear these stories in that context. Your aim is to have at your command a series of stories about Jesus that you can tell easily and well. Practice these. You learn to tell stories well by telling stories often.

The bottom line. The gospel is about Jesus. Jesus is the heart of our message. Jesus *is* the message. Jesus is the one to whom people are

---

[1] I am aware that masculine language is an impediment to some people, and rightly so. For far too long the church talked about God in exclusively masculine language. This is a problem with the English language. We don't have a way of talking about personhood apart from gender language. But it was also a problem of mindset. There are folk who could not imagine women in leadership in the church (despite the fact that Paul sends his greetings to Junias, a woman whom he identifies as an apostle in Romans 16:7) and are very resistant to gender-free language. But in our conversation we need to be as gender-neutral as we can. In this instance I have used the term "Son of Man" and not translated it to gender-neutral language since "Son of Man" is a technical term in the New Testament, filled with a specific content that has nothing to do with gender issues. At other places I will use New Testament terms for Jesus in their original form. Still, we need to strive as much as possible to speak without gender bias, despite the limitations of language.

[2] See my book *Conversion in the New Testament* (Grand Rapids: Eerdmans, 1999), pp. 319-29 for more detail on this strategy.

converted. So we need to learn to tell stories about Jesus taken from Gospel accounts. This will involve us in going back to the familiar stories, studying them in detail, paraphrasing them and then trying them on our friends with the hope that they will want to read the stories for themselves.

1. Have somebody read aloud the story "Heresy" in the resources section (p. 56). Don't follow along with your eyes. Just listen to the story. When the storyteller is finished have him or her read aloud Mark 2:1-12, the Gospel account on which "Heresy" is based. Discuss together the whole experience: how the story affected you, telling Gospel stories as part of a conversation, doing paraphrases of Bible stories and so on.

TRUTH:
How We
Apply It
(15, 25 or 40 minutes)

2. Pick one of the stories mentioned above and try your hand at paraphrasing it for the rest of the group. Take a few minutes of silent work to think about how to tell this story. Then ask a few people to tell their paraphrased stories. Discuss what worked and what did not work.

3. How is your discussion with your conversation partner going?

practice

STUDY   Pick one of your favorite stories about Jesus. Study it thoroughly. Use all the Bible study resources at your command. Then paraphrase it; that is, tell the story in your own words. Write out your paraphrase and then practice telling it aloud.

Over time, do the same thing for other stories until you have a half dozen or so good stories about Jesus that you can tell well.

PRACTICE: Tell the story to your conversation partner. Get his or her reactions
How We Do It   and input.

resources

Heresy: We hadn't had a clear-cut case of heresy for some time. So I was de-
A Story   lighted when reports began filtering down from the north. (Heresy
Based on   was my specialty, and unless one keeps at it, the old touch begins
Mark 2:1-12   to go.)

I chose to investigate this one myself, and we went upcountry to a small fishing village where our suspect was operating.

Luck was with us, and soon after we arrived there was a meeting at his place. We were there, notebooks out. I bet he was pleased when he saw this: Devout followers recording his every word. If he only knew.

Trouble was, I think he did know. I had the uneasy feeling that he knew exactly who we were and why we were there. In fact, I think he made that outrageous statement for *our* benefit. But I'm getting ahead of the story.

It all began when a paralyzed man suddenly appeared in our midst. (That's another story which I won't bore you with at this time.) In any case, the crowd loved it. They hadn't come for the sermon; they wanted action. And here was someone who needed healing.

But he didn't heal him—not right then, anyway. First he made that statement. There he was, quite calm, looking down at the man lying there. Without batting an eyelash he said, "Your sins are forgiven."

I couldn't believe my ears. He was no dullard, you knew that right off. But there he was, saying he had forgiven the paralyzed man's sins when he *knew* that only God could forgive sins. We had him there. That statement was heresy beyond a shadow of a doubt.

But then he looked straight at us and said he knew *we* thought it was heresy. But he didn't think so. Furthermore, he could prove it wasn't. This I wanted to see. If he could get out of this one, the guy was a genius.

But all he did was to ask us a question. "Which is easier," he said, "to heal this man or to say 'Your sins are forgiven'?" He had us there of course. Anyone could say the words "Your sins are forgiven," even me (perish the thought). But healing someone, well that is another story.

Then it hit me like a thunderbolt. I saw what he was getting at. Our theologians (bless their crusty old hearts) had taught "A man gets ill as a punishment for sin he has committed. To recover, his sin must first be forgiven." Any school kid knew that. So if he could heal the paralytic, according to our own theologians he must have forgiven the paralytic's sin.

Well, you can guess what happened; he healed the man. We saw him do it. There he was marching off as proud as he could be with his bed under his arm.

It's out of my hands now; the bureau heads will have to take over the case. You should have seen their reaction to my report. They were hysterical with rage and kept muttering, "But only God can forgive sins."

That troubles me too. I wonder. If only God can forgive sins, what does that make our friend Jesus up there in Capernaum?[3]

---

[3]This article was first published in *His* 30, no. 5. (1970): p. 34, under the title "Heresy Is My Meat."

5

TALKING ABOUT NEED

life

STORY:
Finding Meaning in Life
(5 minutes)

Jerry had it all—a good job (he was now comptroller for the company), a wife who loved him and cared for others, great kids with no problems out of the ordinary. They lived in a big seaside house overlooking the harbor (inherited from his father) in a town that had an outstanding school system. Whatever Jerry touched seemed to turn to gold. Sure he had the minor aches and pains of life—people who were hard to work with, deals that didn't get made, a broken furnace in the middle of winter, fifteen pounds more than his college weight. But he couldn't complain. And he didn't complain. He was grateful—mostly.

But Jerry was restless. At forty-six he had it all in terms of the standards of the time (who sets these standards anyway?), but he still felt a kind of inner emptiness. He didn't know what this was. Mild depression? Unfulfilled longing? Unresolved issues? Mid-life crisis?

Karl Jung, the Swiss psychiatrist, once said that the first half of life is spent making peace with the outer world; the second half is spent making peace with the inner world. What Jerry was feeling is not uncommon for men of his age. He had achieved. He had acquired. He had acquitted himself as a winner, but now he had to deal with the whole question of who he really was and what he was set on earth to do. Inner exploration is not easy, especially for mid-life men.

Jerry probably wouldn't come to Jesus out of a sense of sin and failure. It isn't that he was without sin. He was human like everybody else. It's just that he was haunted by a sense of longing, not afflicted by a sense of failure and wrongdoing.

We sometimes suppose that you can only come to faith via a crisis of conscience. But in fact many people start following Jesus because in Jesus they find the answer to their deepest longings. Jesus calls them to follow him, and so they get involved with a higher purpose and a greater cause. Jesus calls them to care, to give, to serve and to know him, and in so doing to discover their true calling in life.

Jerry is a man who needs to find his calling in life. He needs to discover the cause that will draw forth his unique gifts and special talents. He wants to give (though he only vaguely senses this). He wants to be enlisted in a suprahuman cause. When he comes to Jesus it will be because Jesus meets his need to become more, to be more and to find his true self in God.

In holy conversation one of the questions is, So what? What does all this talk about God have to do with me? For many people the connection is between God and the answer to their deepest longings. To find God is to find meaning in life. So we need to be alert to the issues that enable people to see their need for God.

---

1. What are some of the longings, desires and needs that have shaped your life? How has God used these desires, fulfilled these longings or responded to this need?

LIFE:
How We Live It
(20, 25 or 40 minutes)

2. What are the felt needs and longings of the people you live and work with? What do they want out of life? How are these aspirations connected to God?

3. If Jerry confided in you that he was feeling something was missing in his life, what kind of conversation might you have with him? (If you are feeling bold you might try a role play between one member of your group who takes the part of Jerry and someone else who is a friend of Jerry. Role play is great fun.)

truth

CONCEPT:
*Naming Our
Longing*

(5 minutes)

While some people come to faith out of a need for forgiveness, even more come to faith because Jesus fulfills their deepest longings. Jesus gives us purpose in life. He calls us to engage in bringing his kingdom into being. And his is a kingdom of love. Jesus tells us that the greatest commandment is to love—love God and love others (Mark 12:28-31). This is so simple, and yet it is also so all-encompassing. It is also impossible ever to fulfill fully. This is a challenge worthy of our whole being.

What we really long to find is our true selves. We are men and women created to live in two worlds, the natural and the spiritual. Being rebels against God means that we are cut off from that world of the Spirit. Sure, we have intimations of that other world. We see evidence of the supernatural all around us when we pay attention to such things. But what we really long for is to be reunited with that lost half of ourselves. As St. Augustine reminds us, we are restless until we find our rest in God.

Helping others notice and name these inner hopes, longings and aspirations is a great gift to them. You will have helped them move from a vague sense of disquiet and wondering to awareness that what they long for is God.

So hopes, aspirations and longings are great topics of conversation. This is a very fruitful area of conversation because it resonates so deeply with people in this culture.

These longings take many shapes: the longing to be more and do more, the longing to make a contribution, the longing to find one's true destiny and place in the universe, a longing to make peace with oneself and the world, a longing to make a difference, a longing to know God directly, a longing to be a good person, a longing to have real hope for life after death.

We need to learn to talk about our longings and how God fulfills these. Once again this means that we need to be open and vulnerable about who we are. Our openness will give others the freedom to name their own longings.

Jesus called people to follow him (see Matthew 11:28-29; Mark 1:16-20; Luke 9:23, 57-62). He is still calling men and women to follow him. Often we hear his call by paying attention to our true longings, deep desires and fondest hopes. In holy conversation we can help others notice and name this inner call, even as we seek to be alert to what God is saying to us.

The bottom line. Whereas it is often difficult to talk about our faults and failings, it is much easier to discuss our hopes and aspirations. These longings come from God and direct us back to God. So we need to develop sensitivity to such longings in others and ourselves. And we need to know how to name these longings and how they are rooted and fulfilled in God, beginning by sharing our own needs and longings.

1. In what ways does Jesus fulfill our longings? What has been your experience?

TRUTH:
How We Apply It
(15, 25 or 40 minutes)

2. Explore the whole concept of "calling" and how getting in touch with our true calling in life can also mean getting in touch with who God has made us to be. How can finding our calling also involve finding and following God?

3. How does the church as a community of God's people in mission enable us to work actively on God's agenda? In what ways can the church act as a vehicle for coming to faith by involving seekers as participants in its outreach programs?

4. How did telling the paraphrased story about Jesus go? What did you learn?

practice

STUDY   Make a list of all the outreach activities in which your church engages. How can you invite seeker friends to join in these missions
of mercy and love? What could you do in that context to promote
growth in people's spiritual pilgrimages even as they serve others?

PRACTICE: Talk to your conversation partner about the ways in which you
How We Do It   have found fulfillment of your longings by following Jesus.

resources

Longing   God is written into our very beings. The Bible tells us that we are
all made in the image of God. Children seem to be especially aware
of the reality of God—until we wash out these intimations via the
steady barrage of television, adult indifference and a school system
that teaches other ideas. But those intimations of the divine linger
on deep within us.

They get reinforced by the wonder of the world, which is filled
with the footprints of God—if only we have eyes to see them. But
even the most pedestrian among us gets jarred every once in a while
by a stunning sunset, a majestic snow-capped mountain or a peace-
ful deep-woods lake at dawn. Or we run into the inexplicable: a
friend who seems to have been cured by means of prayer, a conviction we cannot shake that we should do something uncharacteris-
tic, which turns out to have been the right thing though we could
not have known it at the time, or the experience of forgiveness from
someone who, by all counts, should hate us.

Awe, wonder, surprise, love, joy, peace—these all serve to get us
back to that primal sense within us that we were created to be creatures of two worlds—the natural (which is omnipresent) and the
supernatural (which is often so hidden).

And then there are those odd moments when, for a second or
two, it is as if the veil separating the worlds is lifted, and we glimpse

that "other world" and know that this is what we most desire in life.

C. S. Lewis captured this well in a sermon he preached on June 8, 1941 (which was right in the middle of the dark days of World War II). He talks about our inconsolable longing for that other world:

> Apparently, then, our lifelong nostalgia, our longing to be re-united with something in the universe from which we now feel cut off, to be on the inside of some door which we have always seen from the outside, is no mere neurotic fancy, but the truest index of our real situation.
>
> We want something else which can hardly be put into words—to be united with the beauty we see, to pass into it, to receive it into ourselves, to bathe in it, to become part of it. . . . At the present we are on the outside of the world, the wrong side of the door. We discern the freshness and purity of morning, but they do not make us fresh and pure. We cannot mingle with the *slendours* we see. But all the leaves of the New Testament are rusting with the rumour that it will not always be so. Some day, God willing, we shall get *in*.[1]

It is this longing that drives our spiritual curiosity. To understand it, to name it, to see where it is pointing is the challenge. We need others to assist us in this process so that our eyes are opened and we see clearly that we are indeed creatures of two worlds, and then we can begin to satisfy our own inconsolable longing by coming to Jesus who is the bridge to that other world.

---

[1]This sermon, titled "The Weight of Glory," can be found in C. S. Lewis, *The Weight of Glory and Other Addresses* (Grand Rapids: Eerdmans, 1949), pp. 12-13.

6

TALKING ABOUT SIN

life

"You are dirty, rotten sinners; the whole lot of you." We can picture the scene in our minds. A tall, gaunt, dark-clad minister is pointing his bony finger at a group of people who are cringing at his words. They aren't bad people. They just don't match up to the impossibly strict standards of the preacher.

A bleak scene? Yes. An accurate rendering of clergy past or present? Not at all. But nevertheless this image is present in our culture: the harsh, judgmental, religious fanatic who wants to suck the joy out of life.

Unfortunately this colors the way many people think about the whole concept of *sin*. And many people think sin is doing what fanatics think you should *not* do. In other words, sin is merely a matter of definition. "Who is he to tell me what I should or should not do?"

When we do think about sin (which is not often) we take it to be something really gross. It is doing evil things like beating up somebody, cheating on your spouse, robbing a bank or consciously lying about something really important—stuff most of us would never do. So sin is not a word we ever apply to ourselves.

Consequently if we as Christian conversationalists use the word *sin* in our conversation, we invoke all the wrong images. However, the biblical view of sin is much broader and much more comprehensive than either gross evil or breaking unreasonable regulations. So it's really important that when we talk about sin we do so in ways that help others understand what the Bible teaches about sin and not how culture has come to define sin.

Lori is a nice person. Everyone says so. She is always smiling. She never has a bad word to say about anyone. And she is always helping others. But Lori eats too much (though she does most of her binging in secret). Lori's lack of control with food could become the reality through which she comes to understand that she has a sin problem. Once she sees that letting food control her is a form of sin, she may then be able to see that underlying the food problem is a horrid self-image. (In fact, she is nice to people because she desperately wants them to like her.) In reality, she really hates herself. And this is another expression of sin: not loving properly someone upon whom God has lavished love.

Seeing that you need to be freed from and forgiven for your sin is often the first step in coming to Jesus. People won't come to Jesus unless they have a reason to do so. Why bother? Why make all the life changes that commitment to Jesus entails? Often the motivation to come to Jesus is that he will help us with our sin problem. He will bring forgiveness and healing to our lives.

The challenge for us in holy conversation is to talk about sin in ways that connect with people's experience and open up deep insight into themselves while avoiding the cultural misunderstanding of the word. Of course, most of us would rather not talk about sin at all. Why spoil a good conversation? But, alas, you can't understand the gospel without understanding sin. So it's up to us to learn how to communicate this whole idea of sin in a way that is faithful to Scripture and faithful to life and its struggles.

---

1. When you think about the word *sin,* what comes to mind? Which "sins" are the most challenging for you (anger, lust, pride and so on), and how does Jesus help you with this problem?

LIFE:
How We
Live It
(20, 25 or 40 minutes)

2. What do people in your circle understand sin to be all about? Brainstorm together to identify as many expressions of sin (both personal and corporate) as you can. What are some of the ways you can talk to them about sin without using the word?

3. Suppose Lori is your friend. What kind of conversation could you have with her that might help her (and not threaten her) come to grips with her food problem as a way of getting in touch with her sin problem? (Another role play?)

truth

CONCEPT:
Sin as a Description of the Human Condition

(5 minutes)

Sin is really an easy word to talk about without ever using the word itself. There are so many manifestations of sin in our world today: everything from corporate greed, political chicanery and the lack of justice for the people at the bottom of the social order (corporate sins) to personal greed, intemperate behavior and lack of love for others (personal sin). Furthermore, most people have a sense of right and wrong. They know some things are good and some are bad.

But how do you talk about all this without arousing resistance on the part of the other? As Jesus warned us, pointing a finger at others is a sure way to activate their defense and denial systems ("Do not judge, so that you may not be judged"—see Matthew 7:1-5). In any case it isn't our job to bring about conviction of sin in others. That is the work of the Holy Spirit (John 16:8).

What we can do is to talk about our own failings: where we went wrong and did wrong, how we failed and rebelled. However, who likes to talk about personal failure and wrongdoing? Not me. But it's via our personal transparency that others begin to understand sin, guilt and forgiveness. When we share our shortcomings it opens up others to discuss their shortcomings. To name and to own our sins is a key step toward repenting of those sins.

All sin traces its way back to the original sin: human beings turning their backs on God and God's way, and going their own way. But sometimes it takes a while for others to see that they too are rebels against God. The route to this insight may be via owning their own failures and transgressions.

There are lots of words you can use that express the idea of sin—words and phrases such as *failure, losing the way, falling short, shortcomings, flawed, not quite right, wrong, trespassing, twisted, missing the mark, imperfection, breaking the law, evil, wrongdoing, messing up, rebelling, hurting others, making a mistake* and so on. You can think of other words and phrases as well. Use these words in conversation along with being vulnerable and you will lay the groundwork for others to see themselves as they truly are: sinners in need of grace and forgiveness.

But why talk about sin anyway? People don't really believe in sin anymore, so why confuse the issue? Just talk about God's love. Well, the problem is that we have to talk about sin if we are talking about the gospel. "Christ died for our sins" is a central assertion in the Bible. Unless we understand sin, we cannot understand the cross. Unless we understand the cross, we can't really commit our lives to Jesus much less repent and receive forgiveness.

Then there is the issue of motivation. The gospel is all about choosing a new way to live and be. It is about becoming a Christ follower. It is about turning our backs on a life of self-indulgence for a life of loving others. This is just another way of saying it's about choosing to say no to a life in which sin, in one way or another, controls us. *We are motivated to follow Jesus when we discover the high price we pay for sin.* "The wages of sin is death," as Paul reminds us. He goes on to say "but the gift of God is eternal life in Christ Jesus our Lord" (Romans 6:23).

In other words, we only choose Jesus when we see a compelling need or reason to. Nobody changes without a reason to change. All change begins with insight: insight into who we truly are, warts and all, insight into what our life is meant to be over against our deep desire for ease and comfort, insight into how the world works with all of its pain, conflict and death.

So the challenge is to talk about sin without necessarily using the word *sin* and to do so in ways that enable others to understand their own sinful natures and need of repentance.

The bottom line. In order to talk about the gospel we need to talk about sin, but since that word is so misunderstood we have to use other words to get at its true meaning. But understanding the concept of sin is not the real problem; it is understanding that we are sinners in need of forgiveness. The best we can do to help others get to this insight is to be open about our own failures and need of grace, and then pray that the Holy Spirit brings conviction.

1. Discuss sin as

- failure, falling short of the goal, not doing what needs to be done

- transgression, lawbreaking, wrongdoing

- rebellion, going your own way, living only for yourself

TRUTH:
How We Apply It
(15, 25 or 40 minutes)

2. What is wrong with sin, no matter by what name it is known?
    What is the problem of sin? The consequences of sin?

3. What are some of the issues in your life, about which you feel
    free to talk, that might open up others to talk about their issues?

4. What are you learning in your discussion with your conversa-
    tion partner? Give one or two people the opportunity to share.

practice

STUDY   Watch an evening of television and take notes on every example of
sin (in all of its various manifestations) both corporate and personal. What are the "wages of sin" according to television? How do
people grasp the reality of sin and their own personal culpability?

PRACTICE: Keep the conversation going with your conversation partner by
How We Do It   talking about your research into sin. Ask for help in providing examples of sin and its many manifestations both from personal experience and from the media. You can get into a good discussion
about "what's wrong with our country," "the lack of a meaningful
morality" and other such topics.

resources

Sin is one of those words we don't like, and we continually misunderstand. Mostly we conceive of sin as gross misdeeds. It is this, to be sure, but sin is far more domestic than we realize. The word also encompasses all the little things we do—the white lies, the small cruelties, the mundane hostilities. *Sin* is the word that is used to describe wrongdoing in all its forms, big or small, personal or corporate, consciously conceived or unconsciously acted out.

But sin is more than just misdeeds (trespasses); it's also failure (shortcomings). Sin is not just what we do wrong; it's what we fail to do. It is not just bad deeds; it's failure to do good.

The word *sin* is used frequently in the Bible (as everyone knows). But in Greek and Hebrew *sin* is not a single word as in English. There are various words that are translated by this one English word. However, all these biblical words tend to cluster around two core images:

- *The image of transgression.* To sin is to cross the fence and go into your neighbor's forbidden field; sin is stealing that which belongs to another; it's going against God's commandment to love others.

- *The image of shortcoming.* To sin is also like an archer shooting arrows at a target, none of which hit the bull's-eye. They all fall short. To sin, in this sense, is to be unable to live the kind of wholesome life you want to live; it's failing to understand properly what the Bible is saying to you; it's not noticing the hungry and dispossessed in our midst.

If we have trouble when it comes to personal identification with sin as trespass (we really do try to follow God's ways), we have no trouble at all identifying with sin as failure (we are all too aware that we don't always get it right). The Book of Common Prayer speaks of sins of commission (doing evil) and sins of omission (not doing good). Sin is choosing to do wrong, to embrace evil, to relish the bad. Sin is also not getting it right, not doing the right, not understanding the right.

Sin is what needs to be changed in order to grow. This is what insight is all about: the recognition of our sin. This is what repen-

Defining Sin

tance is all about: the decision to deal with our sin. This is what growth is all about: the attempt to move beyond our sin (as best we can).

God and Sin

Yet another aspect of sin needs to be considered. In the eyes of God, sin is not just an unfortunate lapse or an understandable error. Sin is serious, really serious business. Sin creates a barrier between God and us. This is why Jesus came to our planet: to deal with the problem of sin. This is why he died. His death paid the price for our sin. His death opened up the way for us to go back home to God. There are a lot of theories as to why his death had this effect. But all we really need to know and believe is that "God proves his love for us in that while we were still sinners Christ died for us" (Romans 5:8).

One final note. The assurance of forgiveness is what makes repentance possible. The death of Jesus on our behalf makes forgiveness possible. Unless we know that what we see in our lives and name as sin will be forgiven, we won't explore our lives. But because we are assured of forgiveness, we do open ourselves to the insights that reveal who we are, and thus the whole growth process can go forward.[1]

---

[1]This material is taken from Richard Peace, *Spiritual Transformation: Taking on the Character of Christ*, pp. 48-49. 1997 © Richard Peace.

7

TALKING ABOUT REPENTANCE

It is all well and good to know that you are deeply messed up, living a ruined life. It is all well and good that you want to do good for others and so find purpose and fulfillment in your own life. But knowing who you are and what you need is not enough. You have to take the next step. You have to act. *Insight needs to be followed by decision.*

Connie was a drunk. She knew it. Her family knew it. Everybody knew it. But that knowledge didn't stop her from drinking. Tony attended more seminars than he cared to remember on how to find and fulfill your inner longings. He really knew a lot about the interior life. But this didn't make much of a difference in his life. He still felt out of touch with "the way things are," as he put it.

What both Connie and Tony need to do is *repent*. Repentance is making the decision to stop walking along the destructive or unfulfilling path and instead to turn around and start walking on a new path toward wholeness and commitment.

Repentance is the first step beyond insight. It is saying, "Okay, I know I need to change. So I'm going to turn around from this destructive and unfulfilling life. I'm going to turn around from sin and start following the way of Jesus."

The decision to turn around and go a new way (repentance) is a powerful decision. But we can't do it on our own.

So what is the difference between genuine repentance and a New Year's resolution to do better? The answer is the Holy Spirit. Conversion can't take place unless the Holy Spirit is operating in a person's heart and mind. Otherwise what happens is religious coercion or brainwashing. Besides, the change is not permanent. The Holy Spirit is involved from start to finish in the process of conversion:

STORY:
The Decision
(5 minutes)

bringing insight into our sin and need, enabling repentance, giving the gift of faith, and transforming a life via the gift of new birth.

In our holy conversation we need to talk about repentance. But *repentance* is an odd word, not much used in daily conversation. Still, the concept is familiar. Repentance is all about *changing our minds,* about *deciding* to give up a bad behavior and replace it with a better behavior. For example, repentance is deciding to stop smoking and start living in a healthy fashion. So it's possible to talk about repentance even if we never use the word itself. This is what theological translation is all about.

LIFE:
How We
Live It
(20, 25 or 40
minutes)

1. Give an example in your life of repentance: how you faced a hard truth about yourself and made a decision to go a better way.

2. Think of as many examples as possible of "repentance resolutions," that is, of ordinary situations in which choices are made to do better, such as deciding to become a better parent or resolving to give money to the homeless.

3. How does the Holy Spirit operate in hearts and minds to bring about the willingness to change? What is your experience?

truth

CONCEPT:
Defining
Repentance
(5 minutes)

Repentance is not a word we use regularly. It has a slightly archaic sound to it, like something out of the medieval church or perhaps from the tents of revivalists with their sawdust trails. It conjures up images of robed men carrying signs saying "Repent! The World Is Coming to an End." But, in fact, *repentance* is quite a respectable biblical word. It is used literally hundreds of times in the Old Testament (usually in reference to the people of Israel) and scores of times in the New Testament.

Repentance simply means "to change your mind." It is that straightforward. The context of that change has to do with God. To repent is to change your mind about how you are living in relationship to God. Repentance is understanding that all is not well, that you are in fact not walking in God's way. It's deciding to change that state of affairs by turning around and going God's way.

Of course, we can't repent unless we *see* the issues in our lives. Before we can change our minds about how we are *behaving,* we need to see that what we are doing is wrong, inadequate, less than the best or not desirable. Before we can change our *ideas,* we need to understand that they are in error. Before we can adopt a new *attitude,* we need to own that the old attitude is defective. Thus repentance begins with *insight.*

Insight comes in a variety of ways. Sometimes it comes through the comment of a friend that gets us thinking about ourselves. Or perhaps we read a book or see a film in which we find ourselves portrayed. Insight comes from the negative examples of others ("I don't want to be like him"), from inner longings to be better or different, from dissatisfaction with the status quo.

It isn't easy to see ourselves as we truly are. We spend a whole lifetime building up defenses against "seeing." So the question for us is, How can we help people see clearly? On one level the answer is that we can't. We have all we can manage just trying to see ourselves clearly. And the Bible has something to say about the danger of seeing a speck in the eye of your neighbor while failing to notice the log in your own eye. Still, as we witness our friends engaging in self-destructive behaviors, we can long for them to notice, stop and change—for their own health.

How do we talk about repentance in ways that others will understand? This is always the challenge when it comes to witness.

In fact, even though the word *repentance* is strange and little used, the basic idea of repentance is pretty easy to grasp. It has to do with "changing our minds" about how we are living in relationship to God. It's easy to explain.

Or we can use mini images, like the story of the kid who raises hell in high school, drinking and drugging, until he kills another kid while driving drunk and gives up his wild life, volunteering at a feeding program. You know the kind of story I mean. The story in the resources section, "A Driving Concern" (p. 75) is a parable about repentance.

Probably the best way to talk about repentance is just to tell your own story: how you decided to stop _____ (fill in the blank) and start instead to _____ (fill in the blank). The human experience of choosing a new way because it leads to new life is a powerful witness.

The bottom line. Insight into our relationship with God—or better still, our lack of relationship with God—is the first step in the process of conversion. But knowing is not enough. We need to act on our insight. We need to repent, that is, to decide to stop walking away from God and start following Jesus. Usually people begin to think about the need to repent by hearing a story of how others came to themselves and decided to go a new way. So again, transparency is key to holy conversation.

TRUTH:
How We
Apply It
(15, 25 or 40
minutes)

1. How can you be the kind of person that brings insight to others, insight that opens the way to change?

2. What do you want to say to Tony and Connie?

3. What parables, illustrations, songs, films or pieces of art illustrate what repentance is all about?

4. What are you learning in your discussion with your conversation partner? Give one or two more people the opportunity to share.

practice

Write a story, compose a poem or song or research an illustration of repentance. See the parable in the resources section as an example.

STUDY

Ask your friend what image comes to mind when he or she hears the word *repentance*. Talk about repentance together. Tell stories of repentance on your part, a mini-repentance or even major repentance if your relationship is solid enough for such sharing.

PRACTICE:
How We Do It

resources

I wish I wouldn't keep bumping into people. I mean, it's embarrassing apart from anything else. Having to say "sorry" to people, brushing off their clothes, helping them up from the street. Sometimes they even get hurt, really hurt. Like once this middle-aged executive type—you know, dressed in the pinstriped charcoal suit with the leather briefcase—well, he was in the middle of the crosswalk and was looking the other way, watching a beautiful woman or something, and wham, I hit him. Well, he fell hard, and it turns out he broke his arm and all that. Wouldn't you know it, he was a lawyer, so I got sued.

As a result I drive very slowly these days and watch carefully so I won't run into people or things or other cars. But still, it's hard . . . looking over my shoulder and trying to steer straight, and at the same time operating the gas pedal, not to mention the brakes. Driving in reverse is no picnic.

Of course all that might change. At least my friend Mitchell tells me it can. You see he has this weird idea (he's got a lot of weird ideas, I might add, but he's nice) . . . anyway, he tells me that I don't have to spend my life driving in reverse. In fact, he says we weren't meant to go in reverse all the time. The original plan was for all of us to go forward—which, frankly, I find hard to accept, but then I've never been big on metaphors.

"A DRIVING CONCERN":
A Parable About Repentance

So I asked him where he got this idea, and he told me that there is this whole group of people who believe in going forward. They're like a club and they meet every week. They spend a lot of time talking about forward living, and they give out tracts about this to people, one of which Mitchell gave me, I might add. Anyway, some guy who lived a long time ago who first got this forward living idea started this club.

So I said, "What's the big deal. Why go forward in this life. If God had meant us to go forward, he wouldn't have created reverse gear," which I guess was what Mitchell was waiting for me to say 'cause he said that, in fact, if I looked carefully, my car had not only a reverse gear but three forward gears. And, he said, when he tried driving forward himself, he found that the ride was a lot smoother and he could go faster and he didn't bump into people as often.

Well, he had me there. I really don't like the way I've been going, hurting all those people. So maybe, just maybe, I *will* turn around and start going in the opposite direction. I don't know. At least I'm considering it. In the meantime I'm reading this little book Mitchell gave me. It's the words of this guy who started it all. Fascinating stuff. Who knows, maybe there is something to it after all. Jesus seems to know what he is talking about.[1]

---

[1]Credit has to be given to a former student of mine, W. Mitchell Beddingfield, who inspired this parable. He proposed the whole idea of driving in reverse in one of his class papers.

8

TALKING ABOUT CONFESSION

life

Confession often marks the difference between true repentance and wishful thinking.

Remember Connie and Tony of chapter seven? Connie was the alcoholic and Tony was the unfulfilled guy.

The thing that made the difference for Connie was *not* telling herself that *this time* she really was going to quit drinking. She had done that more times than she could remember. (She had once actually stopped drinking, but it only lasted four months.) No, the big difference was that this time she joined an Alcoholics Anonymous group—and in so doing she identified herself as a person with an alcohol problem. She spoke at the meetings: "Hi, my name is Connie, and I am an alcoholic." She had a sponsor whom she called when things got rough. She even told God that she was a drunk and wanted release from her addiction. In short, the difference was that now she owned her problem and started doing something about it by working through the whole AA program, all twelve steps.

And this meant confessing that she was powerless over alcohol and that her life had become unmanageable (step one). It meant believing that God could restore her to sanity (step two). It meant making a decision to turn her will and life over to God (step three). It meant making a fearless moral inventory of herself and then admitting (confessing) to God, to herself and to others the exact nature of her wrongs (steps four and five). It meant being willing to let God change her and then asking God to do so (steps six and seven). *In other words, Connie owned who she really was and gave the problem over to God in repentance and faith via the act of confession.*

Notice how central confession is to the Twelve Step program. Notice too how familiar many of the twelve steps are. This is not an accident. The Twelve Step program is based consciously on New Testament principles of transformation.

For Tony, the difference came when he let go of his pride and his power. It meant admitting (confessing) that he couldn't find meaning on his own, no matter how many workshops he attended. He couldn't bring meaning into his life simply by listening to gurus. He had to let go and let God do this work. So Tony opened himself up to God, to his own powerlessness, to his friend who had walked with him on this spiritual journey. He said, "Okay, God, do what you want in me. I want your way, not my way. I want to follow Jesus." And then he told others about this (confession). The telling others was hard because Tony had become a bit of a guru himself in his circle, given all the seminars he had attended. Incidentally, a lot of what he had learned now took on new meaning for him. Before he had been standing outside assessing the data. Now he was on the inside, and the data assessed him.

Confession is a key step in conversion. *Confession is repentance actualized.*

But how do you talk about confession? Clearly it isn't your place to say to a friend, "Here are the issues I see in your life. You need to name these issues, offer them to God in repentance and ask for forgiveness." Your friend would say, rightly, "Who are you to tell me what's wrong with my life?" In fact, you probably don't want to talk about confession directly at all. What is helpful is simply to talk about the issues in your own life and the power of confession for you. In other words you model confession instead of talking about it. The response of your friend is up to him or her, but by your openness you have given your friend the option and the right to be open with you.

LIFE:
How We Live It
(20, 25 or 40 minutes)

1. What role, if any, did confession (of sin, need or longing) play in your own coming to and following Christ?

2. We live in a more confessional society than ever before. What sorts of things do people confess—to one another, on television, in books and the like? How does this help (or hinder) us in being more open?

3. Who did you first tell that you had become a Christ follower? Describe the experience. (This is confession in the positive sense.)

truth

CONCEPT:
*Noting,
Naming,
Admitting*

(5 minutes)

To see an issue is one thing, to deal with it is another. The dynamics of repentance involve two things: naming and confessing.

We don't really "see" something until we can give it a name. For example we may be uneasy about our relationships. But until we can own that (1) this is my problem (apart from anything else) and (2) it has to do with my anger (or whatever), nothing will change. *Repentance begins with insight that leads to naming the issue.*

There is great power and great freedom in naming the issue. Until we give the issue a name it remains hidden away in the darkness. To name it is to bring it into the light. To bring it to the light is to diminish its power over us. This is a solid New Testament principle. First John talks about bringing things to the light.

We know this in our own experience. As long as we remain in denial about an issue, that issue controls us. Ask any recovering alcoholic. He (or she) couldn't begin the recovery process until he was willing to stand up and say, "Hi, my name is Bill, and I am an alcoholic." This same principle applies to our issues. Until we can name what is wrong we are inhibited in dealing with it.

Often this naming needs to be public. We need to say it to others. The theological word for this is *confession*. Confession is a basic Christian principle that is a key part of the healing process (James 5:16).

We need to confess our sin and need to ourselves and to God. We may also need to confess our problem to appropriate others (i.e., those nearest to us or those harmed by us because of this issue). We not only confess our sin, but we ask for forgiveness (from God and from others). To ask for forgiveness is a key part of the repentance process. Such a confession brings great relief and freedom because we discover we don't have to be bound to our sin any longer. We have begun to deal with it. New life is possible.

We also need to confess that we have come to Jesus. Confessing sin is the negative side of confession (saying no). Confessing Christ is the positive side of the process (saying yes). Both confessing sin and confessing Jesus are necessary for new life in Christ.

So repentance works like this when it comes to conversion: We discern that we are walking away from God (insight). We identify the problem in whatever way we see it (naming). We say this to God and others and ask for forgiveness (confession). And when repentance is coupled with first-time faith in Jesus, we experience conversion. It is that simple—and that hard.

Interestingly, the way we came to Jesus (by repentance) is the same way we grow in Jesus (by continuing to name and confess our issues). So what we ask of others (in evangelism) is what we ask of ourselves—because we know the power of ongoing repentance in our own lives.

The bottom line. Confession is a key part of repentance. Otherwise repentance is just a mind game. The Holy Spirit gives us the power to confess our sins to God and others, and to ask God for forgiveness and new life. When we experience other people who are willing to be open and confess their issues, this gives us the freedom and the strength to do likewise. We need to become open, honest people in our holy conversation.

TRUTH:
How We
Apply It
(15, 25 or 40 minutes)

1. How are the stories of Connie and Tony examples for us of the dynamic of confession? In what ways are the two stories similar? Different?

2. In what ways can you become more confessional in your life, and what impact will this have on your holy conversation?

3. In terms of your relationships, who do you owe the most openness to? What are the appropriate boundaries when it comes to confession?

4. What are you learning in your discussion with your conversation partner? Give one or two more people the opportunity to share.

practice

Reflect on your life in terms of big turning points. Identify the role of insight, repentance, confession and faith at these turning points. Think about how to share these stories in your holy conversation.

STUDY

What do you have to confess to your conversation partner? How can you help him or her to be more open about needs and longings in his or her life?

PRACTICE:
How We Do It

resources

Confession is really an aspect of repentance. Confession is the public part of repentance in which our decision to change moves from the inner realm to the outer realm. We tell another person (or other people) what we have come to see about ourselves and how we want to change. As such, confession is very important. Otherwise repentance remains interior and the dynamics of change are muted due to our inability to bring others into the process.

The Power of Confession

The Power of Naming

In order to share our problem with another person, we need a name for it. In fact, there is great power just in giving a name to the problem. As long as the problem remains in the mists of darkness without much shape or form, it continues to have power over us. But when we bring it into the light, by calling it for what it is, that power begins to diminish. The fact is that unless we come to the point where we look squarely at an issue and name it for what it is, we can't grow. It is that simple.

The Bible gives us many names for the various sins that beset us. The Ten Commandments urge us (1) to have no other gods, (2) not to make graven images of God, (3) not to take God's name in vain, (4) to remember the sabbath and keep it holy, (5) to honor our fathers and mothers, (6) not to kill, (7) not to commit adultery, (8) not to steal, (9) not to bear false witness against our neighbor, and (10) not to covet our neighbor's goods or spouse. These are foundational issues that define for us what we should and shouldn't do. In the New Testament Jesus gives us the Great Commandment. We are to love God and to love others, using proper self-love as the gauge to measure our love. In New Testament terms, sin is the failure to love.

In post-New Testament times there was concern about the so-called seven deadly sins. The original list included envy, anger, pride, sloth, avarice, gluttony and lust. Later on, issues were added such as fornication, dejection and vainglory.

In our own time Karl Menninger, the famous psychiatrist, catalogued a whole variety of sins, based roughly on the seven deadly sins. He speaks of sin manifested as pride (the pride of power, of knowledge and of virtue); the sins of sensuality (lust, fornication, adultery and pornography); the sin of gluttony (food, drinks and drugs); the sins of anger, violence and aggression; the sin of sloth (laziness, indifference, inactivity, unresponsiveness); the sins of envy, greed, avarice, and affluence; the sin of waste, cheating and stealing; the sin of lying; and the sin of cruelty.[1] If all this is not enough you can add deception, arrogance, unfaithfulness, dishonesty, embezzlement, hypocrisy, exploitation, hatred, vindictiveness and bigotry as well as racism, sexism, and fanaticism.

Most of these terms have to do with willful disobedience: doing what we know to be wrong. There are far fewer terms for failure. But the fact is, we do miss the mark in so many ways. We fail to love fully. (A failure to love lies behind so many of our issues in life.) We

---

[1]Karl Menninger, *Whatever Became of Sin?* (New York: Hawthorn, 1973), chap. 8.

fail to see clearly what is happening in our lives. We fail to live up to our God-given potential. We fail to use our gifts. We fail to respond to the need of others. We fail to notice God. We have a failure of nerve, a failure of compassion, a failure of energy, a failure of courage. The list goes on.

Then there are all the *lacks* that afflict us: the lack of insight, the lack of love, the lack of compassion, the lack of motivation, the lack of sensitivity. There are all the relational sins: impatience, anger, jealousy, judgment, haughtiness, condescension and so forth.

The point in all this is not the name, per se, but accurate identification of areas in our lives where growth is needed. These names simply serve as a grid to understand our particular issues. And also they allow us to say precisely what troubles us.

The Power of Denial

We begin by naming the problem to ourselves and to God. But this can be surprisingly difficult to do. It isn't so bad when it comes to ordinary issues like fudging on the facts in a story we related to a friend or playing games on the computer when we were supposed to be writing a report. We can own up to this sort of peccadillo—usually. No big consequences, of course. But major stuff like our persistent arrogance or our infidelity—this is hard to admit. "Not me!" we cry out, as if keeping it in the dark will make it go away.

When it comes to the act of confession itself, we often find ourselves resisting. We don't want to do it. It's okay to admit, in general, that you are a sinner like everybody else. But to name a specific sin—well, that is different. "That is not really necessary is it?" we ask ourselves. We pull back. We want to talk about something else. Our attention wanders.

This is denial rearing its ugly head. Denial is the refusal to admit to having a particular problem. Denial is covering up, hiding, avoiding the issue and pretending it does not exist. Anything but confession. "I can't say the words. I'm not like that," we say to ourselves.

Denial comes in a variety of shapes and forms:

- Minimizing: "The problem is really not so bad."
- Blaming: "If you knew what I have to put up with, then you'd understand."
- Avoiding: "Forget that. Did you hear the story about . . ."
- Rationalizing: "Let me explain why this is not a problem."

- Excusing: "I guess I just needed to relax."
- Accusing: "You have your own problems to worry about."
- Comparing: "I'm not as bad as her."
- Hiding: "I didn't do that. Where did you get that idea?"

It is hard to get through denial to reality. In fact, sometimes it takes a trained professional to get behind our denial. But mostly it takes a sense on our part that God loves us and wants us to grow, that God's posture toward us is one of forgiveness and not condemnation and that unless we own up we will stay stuck—and this harms us.

The Power of Others

But why confess our shortcomings to others? Why not keep these problems to ourselves? Certainly our instinct is toward secrecy and hiddenness. This is an important question.

There are several principles at work here. For one thing, naming an issue to others puts the problem into the public arena. And once it is out there in plain view of others we have a kind of commitment to do something about it. Even if others don't hold us to account (by reminding us that we said we were going to work on an issue), we still feel accountable. We need to do something; we need to get on with it. Second, our friends will hold us accountable (if we let them)! They will assist us (as they are able) in dealing with the issue. They will listen to us as we wrestle with the problem. They will pray with us and for us. Change was never meant to be a private struggle. It was always meant to be a community process. As they assist us, so we assist them. That is what the Christian community is all about: a clinic for recovering sinners in which we all help each other to be conformed to the image of Christ. It isn't surprising that James urges us to "confess your sins to one another and pray for one another so that you may be healed" (James 5:16).

To whom do we name our issue? Certainly we need to name it to ourselves and to God. Sometimes this is enough. We sense God's forgiveness, guidance and power. We go from strength to strength as we move away from the old behavior, attitude or idea to the new behavior, attitude or idea. But at other times this is not enough. We need to name the issue to the appropriate other. Who that is varies. Certainly we owe the most honesty to those closest to us: spouse, then children, then family, then friends—and so the circles of openness radiate outward. Interestingly, we sometimes reverse the whole process. The anonymous bartender or hair stylist hears the most. Presumably their remoteness from our lives gives us safety in disclosure.

Sometimes we may need professional help—a pastoral counselor, a therapist or another trained professional who can help us get at what is going on. At other times it is the person offended (or harmed) who must be consulted and to whom the confession is owed (as long as we don't harm that person by so doing). At still other times a small group of caring others with whom we are in an accountable relationship need to be the ones who hear our story. Sometimes, if the sin was public (or affected the public), the confession needs to be more general.

The principle is clear: we need to move our repentance from within to without and so gain the strength to change that comes from compassionate care given us by others who know what we are struggling with.[2]

---

[2]This section is adapted from chapter seven of Richard Peace, *Spiritual Transformation,* pp. 60-63. Copyright © 1997 by Richard Peace.

9

TALKING ABOUT BELIEVING

life

STORY:
*The Struggle
to Believe in
a Postmodern
World*

(5 minutes)

Faith must be coupled with repentance for conversion to result. It's not enough to own our own sin, need, longing, failure or aspiration for meaning. That's just the starting point. From this inward recognition of our true state we need to turn outward to Jesus to save us. This "turning to Jesus" is what is called faith.

But faith (or belief) is a problem in this postmodern world where Truth (with a capital T) is suspect. We have lost faith that there is some grand overarching Truth that explains reality and to which we can turn for salvation. In fact, *uncertainty* makes more sense to many people than faith.

And yet we are called on to believe in order to come to God. We are asked to believe that God is real, a person (and not just a force) and involved with the world. We are asked to believe that this God of all power loves us—not generically as one of God's creatures but specifically as a man or a woman with a particular name and place in history. We are called on to believe that Jesus is God's Son: God with us, the One who died for us (to bring forgiveness). And then there is the resurrection. We are asked to believe not only that Jesus died for our sins but also that he rose again to bring us new life.

Don had come to the place where he wanted to believe in Jesus, but he was finding this difficult to do. He and his wife had attended a church for some time now. They liked it. They liked the people. They liked the good things the church did for others, including their own children and their community. Don was impressed that all this concerned action was attributed to a desire on the part of the church to follow God's way. But when the church got to the part about Jesus and following him, this is where Don struggled.

It would be nice if Jesus were God incarnate, Don thought, *but how could a contemporary person believe something like that?* Don knew he couldn't believe what he suspected was not true. But was Christianity true? Don had looked at the so-called historical evidence for the resurrection of Jesus. If Jesus had indeed risen from the dead, all the other seemingly improbable claims fell into place. And the proof for the resurrection did seem strong. But still, why didn't God just come out of hiding, as it were, and show himself clearly and unmistakably?[1]

"But he did," his friends from church said. "God did show himself in Jesus. And also God is present in his creation. Just look at the world around you, and you can see the footprints of God all over it." They also talked about answers to prayer, specific experiences they had had that by their cumulative weight didn't seem just to be coincidences. Don wanted to touch God for himself, but believing was hard.

So how do we talk to the Don's of the world?

Mostly we have to realize that we can never convince anyone about Jesus. Only God the Holy Spirit can bring inner conviction. What we can do is talk about *plausibility* (what helps convince us) and *experience* (how we ourselves know God). Then we have to back off and just walk in love with our friends, praying that the Holy Spirit will bring faith.

---

1. What are some of your core beliefs when it comes to Christianity?

2. In your community, among the people you know, what are the impediments to faith? What makes it hard for people to believe? Why do you believe?

3. What struggles have you had to believe? With what do you now struggle?

LIFE:
How We Live It

(20, 25 or 40 minutes)

---

[1]Talking about God in gender-neutral language is challenging. My own compromise is to refer to God mostly without the use of pronouns, but when it becomes too torturous I use the masculine pronouns simply because it draws less attention to itself. This may or may not be an issue with your conversation partner. Talking about the problem with others is the best solution.

truth

CONCEPT:
Faith as Knowledge, Trust and Commitment

(5 minutes)

The formula in the New Testament for conversion is this: repentance + faith = conversion. You can't be converted without faith.

In the New Testament, both *faith* (the noun) and *believe* (the verb) have a cognitive, an affective and a behavioral aspect. Faith is something we hold to be true (knowledge), something we feel (trust) and something we do (commitment).

New Testament faith begins with knowledge. When it comes to conversion we believe certain things about ourselves and about Jesus. We believe that we are wayward children of God: lost, on the wrong path and disobedient. We believe that Jesus is the way back to God. We believe he is the Son of God who died for our sins and rose from the dead to bring us new life. We can't come to Jesus unless we believe in Jesus. We won't come to Jesus unless we believe that we are disconnected from God and need to come back to God. So faith begins with *conviction.* Our minds are convinced that certain things are true (even if we do not fully understand these things).

But then our conviction turns into trust. Trust is the willingness to reach out to God on the basis of what we hold to be true. *Trust* is a relational term. It exists between people. We not only believe that Jesus died for our sins, we trust Jesus with our lives. To use an oft-repeated illustration, we not only believe that the world-famous tight-rope walker can cross Niagara Falls safely while pushing a person in a wheelbarrow, we are willing to be that person in the wheelbarrow.

Because we trust, we act. We commit our lives to Jesus. We act on the basis of what we believe. Because we believe that Jesus is who he claims to be (knowledge) and because we open ourselves to a relationship with him (trust), we actively follow Jesus (commitment). Henceforth we turn our backs on a self-centered way of life and seek to live in accordance with the way Jesus calls us to live. In other words, we act on what we believe and trust. *New Testament faith engages the whole person.*

We use the word *faith* a fair amount in our everyday conversation. But that use of *faith* is insipid in comparison to the New Testament understanding of faith. When we say "Have faith in me" we usually mean something like "Trust me despite your past experience with me and your expectations that I will let you down again." *New Testament faith is far more robust: because we believe Jesus to be who he claimed to be, we are willing to stake our lives on this fact. We give him our allegiance in warm-hearted trust and commitment.*

All this makes sense to contemporary people. Belief is important; trust is crucial, and acting on our convictions is the mark of a consistent human being. The problem is with knowing what to believe when we hold that absolute truth doesn't exist (or it exists but we have no sure way of accessing it). This is an issue. The best we can hope for is to show people the plausibility of our beliefs, and then live in such a way that others see the fruit of our belief.

The bottom line. Talking about faith is an important part of holy conversation. It is important to understand what the New Testament means by faith (knowledge, trust and commitment) over against how our culture understands faith (as a tentative conviction not always in line with the facts). Faith in Jesus is meant to engage us on all levels of our being, including our mind, our heart and our obedience.

1. What difference does your faith in Jesus make in who you are, what you believe, how you trust and the way you live? How can these realities become part of your holy conversation?

TRUTH:
How We
Apply It
(15, 25 or 40 minutes)

2. Discuss together the difference between how the word *faith* is used in the New Testament and how the word is used in ordinary conversation. How can we help others to see the differences between the two understandings? How can we use the cultural understanding of faith as a way to talk about faith in Jesus?

3. What is the difference between proof and plausibility; between evidence and indicators?

4. How open have you been able to be with your conversation partner about your life and faith? Discuss this experience.

practice

STUDY Continue your reflection on the difference faith makes in your life. Think about what you believe and why you believe it, how you would live if you did not believe, and how knowledge, trust and commitment intersect in your life. What incidents in your life display what you believe and how belief affects you?

PRACTICE: Talk to your conversation partner about how faith makes a differ-
How We Do It ence in your life.

resources

Faith and Our friends may struggle with this call to faith in Jesus. "How do
Credulity we know these things to be true? What evidence is there that Jesus is who he claimed to be?" Depending on the mindset of the one who asks the question, we can go in one of two directions.

For some people, especially the older generation, what they want is proof. "The facts, just give me the facts." So give them what they want. There is ample apologetic literature available. Apologetic literature argues the case for Christianity. Loan them a copy of *Basic Christianity* by John Stott.[2] This book has been in print for a long time now. It has sold two and a half million copies so it obviously connects with people. *Basic Christianity* makes the case for Jesus with great power and persuasion. The arguments in that book are ones that each of us should master and make part of our own conversations.

Others want a way to validate the truth of all this in their own experience. Such folk (we call them postmoderns) distrust truth claims of any sort, feeling that truth is in the eye of the beholder. For these folks, do two things. First, invite them to join you in your faith community. Invite them to experience God in your worship service, to study the Bible with you, to join you in acts of service, to hang out with you as you hang out together. The truth they need is the truth of the community of God's people. Second, invite them to reach out to Jesus and see what happens. Invite them to trust Jesus as much or as little as they can. Invite them to pray. Invite them to read the Gospels to access firsthand the story of Jesus. Invite them to test in their own lives the truth of what you are saying and have experienced in your life.

Sometimes *faith* is defined as "believing what you know is not true." You hear this less these days because we have come to understand that reality is not defined solely by what we see with our eyes, touch with our hands or hear with our ears. Modern physics alone has pushed the boundaries of reality beyond the mere empirical. But still, it is true that we can't really direct our faith toward that which we suspect is fictitious, even if it is a pious lie that makes us feel better. Even postmoderns opt for authenticity. So struggle alongside your friends as they struggle to know.

---

[2]John Stott, *Basic Christianity* (Downers Grove, Ill.: InterVarsity Press, 1959).

10

TALKING ABOUT
BELIEVING IN JESUS

life

STORY:
*Why Believe
in Jesus?*

(5 minutes)

The Christian faith is not about faith in a generalized sense. Just "believing" is not enough. We believe in all sorts of things that make no difference whatsoever in our lives. Conversion involves *believing in Jesus*. It's the content of our faith that is crucial, not just that we have faith.

But why Jesus? Why not the Buddha? Why not faith in the goodness of humanity or the power of love? Why be so specific?

Hetty believed in lots of things. She believed that God loved her, that she had a special role to play in this life, that God's energy and love pulsated through this planet, that the most important thing was being good and loving others. She believed in many other things as well. But one thing she did *not* believe was that Jesus was the One, God's child come to save his lost people. That was so narrow. It excluded.

Her Christian friends told her that believing in Jesus was just aligning herself with the way things are. They said that Jesus loved everybody and wanted all people to be part of the kingdom of God.

"Thank you very much," she said, "but I prefer to do it my way."

But Jesus does make a difference. He's not just another religious leader who teaches wise and true things. He claims to be God's only Son. And he's not just "the son of God" in the sense that we are all children of God. He is God-come-in-the-flesh: the mighty God of the universe incarnated as a human being. He claims to have the power to forgive our sins and give us the gift of eternal life. Furthermore, Jesus is alive, and we can be in relationship with him. And this is a relationship that is real, immediate and makes a difference. We can know Jesus, and we are changed by this experience.

So the question is how do we believe in Jesus in a holistic New

Testament way? What does it mean to focus our faith on Jesus? What are we called on to believe with our minds? How can we reach out in trust to Jesus? And what does commitment to him look like?

Of course, the challenge is to talk about this with others. The challenge is to stay true to what we have come to know and believe without being doctrinaire, intolerant and unloving. In holy conversation our goal isn't to challenge the beliefs of others. Our goal is just to make what we believe about Jesus clear, convincing and plausible.

----

1. When did you first believe in Jesus, and what difference has this made in your life?

LIFE:
*How We
Live It*
(20, 25 or 40 minutes)

2. Explore the resistance in our society to believing in Jesus. What are the ways that we can talk with others about this without being defensive or overbearing?

3. Who do your friends believe in, and why?

What do we mean when we urge others "to have faith in Jesus"? We have discussed the "have faith" side of the issue (chap. 9), but what about the "in Jesus" part? Faith is important, but the object of our faith is even more important. What matters is not just that we believe but in what or in whom we believe. Faith is not an abstract "feeling" (as pop culture would have it). Faith has a direction to it. Having faith *in Jesus* is at the very center of what it means to be a Christian. But what does it mean to have faith in Jesus?

CONCEPT:
*How to
Believe in
Jesus*
(5 minutes)

First, when we use this phrase we mean by it that *Jesus is worth believing in.* He is who he claims to be: the divine Son of God come in human flesh. He is God with us. He is God come to our planet to reveal to us the true nature of God. Therefore his words are true in an absolute sense. They can be trusted. He is true. He can be trusted. We *believe* him to be the Son of God and thus *trust* in him as the Lord of our life even as we *obey* his commandments.

Second, we mean that *Jesus is worth trusting.* He died to save us from our sin. He did something so amazing that we can scarcely grasp its significance. By his death he made it possible to come home, to come back to God, back to God's kingdom. Not only that, he rose again from the dead to give us new life. He offers us his resurrection life. This isn't ordinary life; this is eternal life that begins in the here and now and extends beyond the grave. By faith we trust in the death and resurrection of Jesus. In other words, we *believe* that he died for our sins and gives us new life, so we now *trust* Jesus for that forgiveness and new life, and we *follow* his path toward fullness of life.

Third, we mean that *Jesus is worth following.* To have a relationship with Jesus involves a commitment to his way. "If you love me, you will keep my commandments," Jesus tells us (John 14:15). Following Jesus is not odious. In fact, by following Jesus we discover life at its fullest. Jesus leads us in the way of truth, love and transformation. We *believe* Jesus is the way; we *trust* him to lead us is the path of wholeness, and we *commit ourselves* to his way. This is what it means "to have faith in Jesus."

The bottom line. Belief is at the very heart of conversion. But this isn't generalized belief. It's belief in Jesus. It's belief that he died for our sins and rose to give us new life. It's belief that by turning to him we can be forgiven of our sins and will experience new life. Belief in Jesus is quite different from belief in anything or anyone else.

TRUTH:
How We
Apply It
(15, 25 or 40
minutes)

1. What is the nature of your faith in Jesus, and how might you talk about this to others?

2. What does it mean to believe in Jesus? How is this different from believing in anyone or anything else?

3. What would you say to Hetty?

4. What are you learning in your discussion with your conversation partner? Give one or two people the opportunity to share.
   (In this session and the next make sure each small group member has had at least one opportunity to talk about what has been
   learned from his or her conversation partner.)

5. You have two more sessions left in your small group. Begin planning a farewell party following the final session. Who will bring
   what? Do you want to invite your conversation partners to join
   in this final session?

practice

Explore what you believe about Jesus. What beliefs are central?
What beliefs are secondary? How does such belief affect your life?

STUDY

- -

Continue your conversation about faith and the difference this
makes in your life, focusing specifically on your faith in Jesus.
What would your life be like without your unfolding relationship
with Jesus?

PRACTICE:
How We Do It

resources

Defining
Faith

Let's examine in more detail the three aspects of the word *faith* as we explore how to talk about New Testament faith in a way that is both faithful to the New Testament and understandable to our seeking friends.

First, there is *the cognitive aspect of faith*. We understand this aspect best via the word *believe*.[1] To believe something is to understand it to be true. "I believe that the sun rises everyday, that my wife is beautiful and that 2 + 2 = 4." All of these are cognitive concepts. That the sun rises is a matter of experience. Every day that I have been alive the sun has risen even when I couldn't see it directly. That my wife is beautiful is an aesthetic intuition: I know in my heart that who she is and how she looks is a matter of beauty. That two apples plus two apples means I have four apples in the bag is a matter of learned experience: teachers taught me arithmetic and the truth of adding and subtracting has been verified in real life.

We believe a lot of different things. No big deal. Everybody does. Some of what we believe is certainly true; other beliefs are more a matter of opinion than hard facts; still other beliefs are factually wrong but psychologically true; and some beliefs are just plain wrong—a product of bad information, wishful thinking, superstition or stupidity.

Beliefs live in our heads. They are matter of the mind. It's important to believe true things because our beliefs make a difference in how we live.

Second, there is the matter of *the affective side of faith*. We understand this aspect best via the word *trust*. Trust is all about believing something deeply enough that we make it part of our lives. It isn't just that we believe something to be true; we let that truth shape us. We believe Jesus to be our Lord and Savior, and so we trust our lives to him.

Trust moves us to a different level. It is relatively easy to believe all sorts of things. But when we act on those beliefs they move from

---

[1]As has been pointed out, in the New Testament *faith* is the noun and *believe* is the verb. I am using *belief* here not as the active form of New Testament faith. Rather, I am using it to identify the cognitive aspect of New Testament faith simply because this is the best English word to get at this aspect of faith.

head to heart. Faith is not disinterested belief. Because we have come to hold certain facts about Jesus to be true, we reach out to Jesus in relationship. We believe in our heads that by his death and resurrection he brings salvation to us. So in our hearts we trust that this is so for us. It is no longer "Jesus is the Savior of the world." Now it becomes "Jesus is my Savior."

But there is a third aspect: *the behavioral side of faith.* We understand this aspect best through the word *commitment.* It's one thing to develop a relationship with Jesus; it's another to walk in his way. There are those people who believe in Jesus as the Son of God, the Savior of the world. They seek to have a relationship with Jesus. But it all stops there. Whatever the nature of their relationship, it stays interior. It doesn't affect how they live. They may feel differently, but they act in the same old ways.

We are warned about this in the book of James. The shorthand way of describing the problem is to say, "Faith without works is dead." By this James means that genuine faith has this third quality to it: it changes how we live. The most obvious way this is seen is in how we love other people. The great commandment given by Jesus is that we are to love God and love others. It's that simple and that challenging. So it isn't enough to profess belief in and trust of Jesus. Our life needs to change because of our belief and trust. It's a matter of *obedience* to Jesus, whom we have named as Lord of our life. Not that we have to become perfect. But in some way, albeit small and growing, we behave differently because of our faith in Jesus.

So in your holy conversation you will want to touch on all three aspects of faith: belief, trust and commitment. Not that you will get into a highly nuanced conversation about the definition of faith. Rather your aim is just to hold up these three parts of faith in some way as your friend seeks to grasp the meaning of faith.

11

TALKING ABOUT COMMITMENT

life
_____

STORY:
How Do I Commit Myself to Jesus?

(5 minutes)

Jan was convinced. She had hung out with her new Christian friends long enough to realize that they had found something real. Jesus was alive for them and made a discernable difference in their lives. She wanted this for herself. So, how did she do it? What was involved in becoming a bona fide follower of Jesus?

She asked Marti about this. Marti seemed delighted that Jan wanted to follow Jesus, but she was vague about the details. "Well, you believe in Jesus, don't you?" Marti asked. Jan assured her that this was the case. She believed all the things the others at church seemed to believe: that Jesus was the Son of God who had come to earth, suffered, died for our sins, was raised from the dead—all those assertions in the creeds.

"Well, what about sin?" Marti asked. Jan laughed. "Marti, Marti, you of all people know me well enough to know what a disaster my life has been when it comes to playing by the rules. Do I need to be healed and forgiven? Of course. That's what started this whole Jesus business for me. But I've turned my back on my old life, mostly, and I have started to live the way Jesus calls me to live. I have a long way to go, but I am pointed in the right direction."

"Okay, I guess that's it. You are as much a Christ follower as anybody," Marti concluded.

But somehow this didn't feel right for Jan. She thought about her marriage. Before she and Jim actually got married they knew they loved each other. They spent lots of time together. They counted themselves a "couple" and were faithful to one another. But when she walked down that aisle one day, with all their friends watching, and exchanged vows with Jim, a whole new reality began for her.

Was there a way that she could declare her commitment to Jesus?

There are two issues here. First, what does it mean to commit your life to Jesus? And second, how does a person "declare one's colors," as it were? Is there a ritual or an action by which someone says to the world, "Now I follow Jesus"? On both these issues Jan needs good counsel.

When it comes to holy conversion, what can you say about the process of commitment? In the past Christians have talked about the metaphor of opening the door of your life to Jesus, who is knocking or praying the sinner's prayer. But I think there are more useful ways to talk about commitment (see the "Truth" section below).

1. What did your "act of commitment" to Jesus look like? Or how did you know that you had at that point become a follower of Jesus?

LIFE:
How We Live It

(20, 25 or 40 minutes)

2. What would you say to Jan?

3. What does "conscious commitment" bring to a person's life? Why is it important?

So how does a person actually become a follower of Jesus? What are the steps of commitment? How do you say yes to Jesus?

The theological answer is that to become a Christian or Christ follower:

- you sense a need or longing in your life that only God can fulfill,

CONCEPT:
Saying Yes to Jesus

(5 minutes)

or you are convicted of your sin which only God can forgive (insight)

- you respond by deciding to turn from the sin or failure to Jesus (repentance)
- you admit this to God, yourself and others (confession)
- you reach out to Jesus (by faith)

But what does this look like in actual practice?

The traditional answer is that you "pray the sinner's prayer," in which you confess your sin, ask for forgiveness, profess faith in the saving power of Jesus and say that you commit your life to Jesus.

But to postmodern people all this seems rather too mechanical, as if coming to God were a magical incantation that if followed produces magical results. But Christianity is a relationship, not a formula.

This is why we need to talk about commitment in relational terms (coming into relationship with Jesus), not just in ideological terms (believing certain things about Jesus).

What does it mean to begin a relationship with another person? Well, first you have to *want a relationship* with that other person. There is an attraction to the other; there is a resonance within you with the other. (In terms of conversion this is another way of saying that you recognize a need or longing in your life that only God can meet.) So you spend time with the other: you hang out together both informally and formally. (You read your Bible and learn about Jesus and his way; you talk to others about Jesus; you join with others to worship Jesus.)

There comes a time when you decide that this is a relationship you wish to sustain—forever. (Or maybe it is more a matter of being drawn powerfully into this new relationship by needs, longings, love, wonder, hope.) In any case, just as in marriage it's important to name (own/submit to/agree to) what you desire ("Will you marry me?") and formalize the fact ("With this ring I thee wed"). It is important to own the moment, to have a formal declaration of commitment. (Such a consciousness of commitment is often the difference between a nominal Christian faith, which does not result in much transformation of life, and a vital Christian faith that sits at the center of who we are.)

The marriage metaphor, though sanctioned by Scripture, may or may not be helpful—given a person's relational history. For many people the metaphor of "coming home" expresses better how they came into relationship with Jesus. In fact, the story of the prodigal son may be the best illustration in the New Testament of what it means to come to commitment to Jesus. (See the resources section on pp. 103-5.)

The church has developed rituals by which to express your commitment to Jesus. In some churches this involves "going forward" at the end of a service to declare your desire to follow Jesus. More liturgical churches have a service of confirmation, whereby young adults claim for themselves the commitments made on their behalf, in baptism when they were infants. The service of adult *baptism* is another of these ritualized events whereby we say publicly that we are Christ followers.

Even though conversion is a process for most people, it's important to bring that process to a successful conclusion. Thus we need metaphor and ritual whereby individuals give themselves to a relationship with Jesus.

I need to say one more thing about commitment. Many people who are sincere followers of Jesus can't point to any one time or event when they became a Christian. They know that at one stage in their life they didn't believe in Jesus, but now they do. But they can't trace the arc between these two stages. Other people grew up in the church and always believed in Jesus. Still others committed themselves in various small ways to Jesus over time, which seem to have resulted in their becoming committed Christians. So the important thing is not how or when you started following Jesus but that you now are consciously following him.

The bottom line. Conversion needs a conclusion. A process that never ends is ultimately futile. So we need a way of talking about commitment. The metaphor of marriage or the story of the prodigal child can function in this way. We also need rituals by which to mark out such commitment so that what is private becomes public. In this way we are called on to name our new allegiance to Jesus and thus begin actively to follow his way.

---

1. Discuss the various rituals by which we express our commitment to Jesus (coming forward, baptism, confirmation, joining a church, etc.). What are their strengths? Weaknesses?

TRUTH:
How We Apply It
(15, 25 or 40 minutes)

2. How can we help our friends come to commitment?

3. What is the problem with conversion as a never-ending process?

4. Sum up what you have learned about conversation from you conversation partner.

5. Finish planning the final celebration.

practice

STUDY   Imagine that a friend asks you, "How do I become a follower of Jesus?" Think about what you might say to him or her using the prodigal son story (see pp. 103-5) as the basis of your response.

PRACTICE: Tell the story of the prodigal son (or daughter) to your conversation
How We Do It   partner this week. Make it live as a good story. Fit your story into that story. See what happens.

resources

There is a wonderful story in the Gospel of Luke that describes in a powerful way what it means to come home to God. It is a metaphor that resonates deeply with us and, as such, describes how we open our lives to God in repentance and faith. It is Jesus who first told this story, so it has his stamp of approval as a way of describing commitment to God.

COMING HOME: *The Prodigal Son as a Metaphor for Commitment*

I am referring, of course, to the story of the prodigal son. We all know the story (found in Luke 15:11-32). Each episode (or act) in this story describes a key feature of the spiritual journey back home to God.

Act one of this story begins, as do all good stories, with a problem, a challenge, a dilemma. The younger of the two sons is bored with home. He demands his inheritance so he can live his own life. And amazingly his father grants his audacious request. The property is divided up, and the younger son gets a hunk of cash.

It sounds a lot like our story. We are the beloved children of a wise and loving God who allows us the freedom to leave home and make our own way in life. He doesn't hold us without our consent. In fact, he gives us great and abundant gifts of all sorts: health, strength, skills, energy, creativity and so on. Even though we chose to leave his way and his kingdom, God knows that this, our true home, is planted deep in our hearts. And that longing for our true home will stay with us no matter what.

Act two finds the young man engaged in what the text calls "wild living"—wine, women and song, literally. And what do you know, his money soon runs out, after which so do all his new friends. And this happens when the country in which he has been living experiences a severe famine. The prodigal (for this is what he is) now tastes the bitter fruit of a ruined life. He is "in need" as the text says, alone, feeding pigs (remember what pigs meant to the Jews), hungry and without hope.

Again, there are a lot of parallels to our own situation. We misuse our freedom, our capital and our good gifts. Seeking pleasure we find only famine. What once seemed so glamorous is now turned to ashes. And we are sad, sorry and in need. What a great picture of sin and its consequences we find in the experience of the prodigal.

In act three the prodigal "came to his senses." He faces his true reality: he is in a pit, at the bottom, lost. But he remembers his home. He longs to be back there where he belongs, except he knows that he gave up all that. He renounced his role as a son. He wonders if he can become a hired servant for his father and live on the edges of his old life. He will confess to his father his sin and ask for a little mercy.

This is what repentance and faith are all about, aren't they? Repentance begins with understanding our true situation: no illusions, no denial, just the cold, hard facts no matter how bad they are. Repentance then moves to decision: the choice to turn around and go the other way, to return home, to leave that far country. Repentance ends with confession—confession of all this to the one against whom all sin is ultimately focused: God. Faith enters in because we believe we will be allowed back, that we are still loved and that there is a way to return home, despite what we have done. Without faith, repentance would be impossible. So as prodigals we turn our back on our sin and reach out to Jesus in faith.

Act four is the welcome. And what a welcome it is! The father spots the prodigal a long way off and literally runs out to meet him. The father is filled with love and joy. The confession that the prodigal has been working on is made, but the father is hardly listening. Instead he is planning the grand banquet to welcome back his son. The prodigal may have thought he had lost his birthright, but to the father he is still the beloved son—once lost, now found; once dead, now alive again.

Salvation is like that. As we reach out to God in repentance and faith we find that God is already there. God has always been there, waiting for us with love and acceptance. And so we are welcomed home and celebrated in our return. How wonderful! How amazing!

But there is one more act. Remember there were two brothers. The older brother stayed home, served his father, worked hard and kept the rules. And he is furious that this prodigal brother of his gets a grand party after squandering half the family holdings with prostitutes and wild living. His father reminds him of what is true and always has been true: that everything the father has is his. He tries to draw the older brother into the celebration.

A lot of us are like the older sibling. We have kept the rules (mostly), done the right thing (usually), worked hard (generally) and tried to be upstanding citizens (at least publicly). But we didn't do all this with much grace. We envied the prodigal even as we disdained him and his ways. We lived on the side of rules but lost our joy along the way. We too need to be drawn back. Not back home so much as back to the joy, love, life and spirit of our home, all of which somehow got lost for us.

So this story is not only about those who have wandered far from God and want to come back home. It is also about those who have stayed home but with resentment. Both the prodigal (the seeker) and the elder child (the evangelist?) have a place in this story, so once again evangelism is not a matter of us and them. It is a matter of both of us opening ourselves to the love and joy of God.

PUTTING IT ALL TOGETHER

12

HOLY CONVERSATION

life

For Jake, it was his back injury that got him into what he called his "alternative living" phase. To get some relief from the pain, he started seeing a massage therapist twice a week. It helped, as did the health foods his therapist recommended. At the health food store he met Sarah. Sarah invited him to her group that met weekly to talk about health and consciousness. It was there that he got connected to this whole network of people who pursued alternative ways of living, including meditation, exercise, new ways of eating and (what interested Jake the most) new ways of connecting with the spiritual.

Jake became a seeker. His weekends were taken up with seminars and retreats. He started attending concerts by New Age musicians. He read books about the new consciousness and about ancient forms of spirituality. Jake was sincere. He was deeply interested. He was on a quest.

In the meantime Sarah got converted to Christ. And she started talking to Jake about what happened to her. At first Jake was a bit put off. Where was the old Sarah who started him on his own pilgrimage? But the more they talked, the more Jake got intrigued. His friend Sarah was still there in the midst of her enthusiasm about Jesus. If anything, a new, deeper side of her emerged. It was as if in finding Jesus she found herself.

She wasn't pushy in her views. In fact, Jake had the feeling she was trying out some of her new ideas on him, getting clarity even as they talked. And she didn't have all the answers either. At times she was at a loss for words. Jake raised real issues for her, and she went away and checked them out. And so the conversation continued.

There was something very real at the core of Sarah's experience. It was real for her friends too. In typical Sarah fashion she invited Jake along to her new group. Going to church was still a bit much

STORY:
Pilgrimage to Jesus
(5 minutes)

for Jake, but he did come with her to the Bible study group. He was interested, very interested.

Over time Sarah would learn more about her faith and how to talk about it. Over time Jake would get more and more immersed in this Christian community. Over time he would find Jesus, and so his spiritual journey would take on new character as he learned about the way Jesus called him to live. And he too would become a holy conversationalist.

This is, of course, the goal of holy conversation. To help others find Jesus and so find new life. May it be so in our holy conversation.

LIFE:
How We Live It

(20, 25 or 40 minutes)

1. Sum up what this experience of holy conversation has been like for you and your friends over these past weeks?

2. What is your goal now in the weeks and months ahead when it comes to holy conversation?

3. In what ways does the conversation between Jake and Sarah resonate with your experience of holy conversation? In what ways is it different?

truth

CONCEPT:
Good Conversation

(5 minutes)

So what is holy conversation?

For one thing, holy conversation is just that, *conversation*. It happens between people who know and respect each other. It isn't a one-time event but takes place in bits and pieces over time. It is multifaceted—touching on all sorts of matters. It is filled with give and take. The conversation partners are honest with one another—about what they know and don't know, about their intentions in the conversation, about their experiences.

True conversation is seldom linear, that is, beginning with a concept and then step by step demonstrating the truth of that idea. In fact, conversation is more often about life and experience than about concepts and ideas, though there are some key ideas that need to be talked about since they shape and guide experience.

For another thing, holy conversation is about *holy* issues. It's not random conversation, but it's about the meaning of life, the nature of reality and the existence of God. It's conversation with a focus. In fact, the *content* of the conversation sets holy conversation apart from other conversations. For a Christian the focus of holy conversation is Jesus: who he is, what he has done, how he brings us back to God, how to connect with Jesus.

To be a good conversation partner it's important to remember the rules of conversation. Be kind and generous. Enjoy dialogue. Expect differing views. Be clear in what you say. Be honest. Know that conversation takes place over time. Try to be compelling in what you say about Jesus but not manipulative. Tell stories—lots of stories: stories about him, stories about yourself and stories about God.

To be a good conversation partner you have to take seriously the worldview and the experience of your friends. Your aim is not to demean, deny or disregard their experience or perspective. Likewise you need to take seriously your own experience and knowledge, and not mute or alter it. Remember it isn't you who converts people. It is the Holy Spirit. Your role is to be clear, forthright, honest and knowledgeable.

Especially you need to be knowledgeable about Christianity in order to be a good conversation partner. This is what this training course is all about: understanding the gospel with new depth and learning to talk about it in accurate ways.

Your attitude to your conversation partners is also crucial. If you don't treat them with love and respect, the conversation won't go far. Your words will be contradicted by your attitudes. If you come across as arrogant or judgmental you won't be heard.

When possible, draw your friends into your Christian community. Witness was never meant to be a solitary occupation. In fact, more and more these days conversion takes place in the context of community. Men and women start hanging out with Christians, sharing their activities, their conversations, their fellowship and their worship. Over time they come to understand, accept and experience the gospel that forms the core of this community. The holy conversation that began between two friends is now enlarged via your community of faith where it is experienced in new ways.

Holy conversation isn't meant to be a one-time monologue during which you give your testimony, share a plan of salvation and invite people to commit themselves to Jesus. It's meant to be part of an ongoing relationship. It's meant to be part of your lifestyle. It's meant to reflect who you are and what you value at the deepest level. Holy conversation should become part of your regular conversation: uncontrived, fresh, reflecting your ongoing experience of God and deepening understanding of the gospel. To be a witness is simply to be honest in your day-by-day conversations with others. If God is real to you, then you will talk about that reality. Learning to be a holy conversationalist is learning how to talk about these deep realities.

And in the end you must trust God with the results. God loves your friends in a deep and individual way. God's the one who gently pushes them along in their spiritual pilgrimages (as God pushes you along). Your role is to be a good friend to others and so to share what you know and experience of God. This is an important and necessary role. May you be blessed in your role as a holy conversationalist.

The bottom line. Holy conversation consists of good conversational skills coupled with content focused on the gospel. The rules of good conversation connect people together in love and respect and keep the conversation going over time. The content of holy conversation keeps that conversation focused on Jesus in all his many aspects. Our goal is be competent and knowledgeable conversationalists even as we trust God to work in the lives of our friends as well as in our own life.

TRUTH:
How We Apply It
(15, 25 or 40 minutes)

1. From your experience, what are the rules of good conversation?

2. So what is holy conversation when all is said and done?

3. End your small group study with prayer and celebration. What has the experience of the small group been like for you? What were the high points? The low points? What is next for you? Have a party.

Discuss your experience of this course with friends inside and outside the church.

STUDY

In the end, holy conversation is as much an attitude to conversation as anything. It's the willingness in our daily conversation to be open about our faith and honest about our experience of God. In the coming weeks and months seek consciously to be that kind of conversationalist.

PRACTICE:
How We Do It

A Summary of Key Concepts

1. Spiritual Pilgrimage

The task of evangelism is to help others come to the place in their spiritual pilgrimage so that they are able to hear Jesus' call to them to become his disciples. However, people often need to wrestle with a variety of questions and challenges before they reach this point. Our call is to walk with them on their journey of faith even as we share with them our own ongoing journey of faith.

2. Stories of the Presence of God

In order to engage in holy conversation we need to learn to tell our own stories of God. We need to recall various incidents, both big and small, in which we experienced the aliveness of God. Then we need to craft these into good stories that will fit into our ordinary conversation.

3. Good News

Holy conversation revolves around the gospel, so it is crucial that we have a good understanding of the content of the gospel and that we can talk about it in nontheological terms. The central focus of the gospel is Jesus. We need to learn to talk about him. The death of Jesus deals with the problem of sin. We respond to Jesus through repentance and faith. The outcome is commitment to Jesus.

4. Jesus

The gospel is about Jesus. Jesus is the heart of our message. Jesus *is* the message. Jesus is the one to whom people are converted. So we need to learn to tell stories about Jesus, taken from Gospel accounts. This will involve us in going back to the familiar stories, studying them in detail, paraphrasing them and trying them out on our friends with the hope that they will want to read the stories for themselves.

5. Need

Whereas it's often difficult to talk about our faults and failings, it's much easier to discuss our hopes and aspirations. These longings come from God and direct us back to God. So we need to develop sensitivity to such longings in others and ourselves. And we need to know how to name these longings and how they are rooted and fulfilled in God, beginning by sharing our own needs and longings.

6. Sin

In order to talk about the gospel we need to talk about sin, but since that word is so misunderstood we have to use other words to get at its true meaning. But understanding the concept of sin is not the real problem. The problem is understanding that we are sinners in need of forgiveness. The best we can do to help others get to this insight is to be open about our own failures and need of grace, and then pray that the Holy Spirit brings conviction.

7. Repentance

Insight into our relationship with God—or better still, our lack of relationship with God—is the first step in the process of conversion. But knowing is not enough. We need to act on our insight. We need to repent, that is, decide to stop walking away from God and start following Jesus. Usually people begin to think about the need to repent by hearing a story of how others came to themselves and decided to go a new way. So again, transparency is key to holy conversation.

8. Confession

Confession is a key part of repentance. Otherwise repentance is just a mind game. The Holy Spirit gives us the power to confess our sins to God and others and to ask God for forgiveness and new life. When we experience other people who are willing to be open and confess their issues, this gives us the freedom and the strength to do likewise. We need to become open, honest people in our holy conversation.

9. Believing

Talking about faith is an important part of holy conversation. It's important to understand what the New Testament means by faith (knowledge, trust and commitment) over against how our culture understands faith (as a tentative conviction not always in line with the facts). Faith in Jesus is meant to engage us on all levels of our being, including our mind, our heart and our obedience.

10. Believing in Jesus

Belief is at the very heart of conversion. But this is not a generalized belief. It's belief in Jesus. It's belief that he died for our sins and rose to give us new life. It's belief that by turning to him we can be forgiven of our sins and will experience new life. Belief in Jesus is quite different from belief in anything or anyone else.

11. Commitment

Conversion needs a conclusion. A process that never ends is ultimately futile. So we need a way of talking about commitment. The metaphor of marriage or the story of the prodigal child can function in this way. We also need rituals to mark out such commitment so that what is private becomes public. In this way we are called on to name our new allegiance to Jesus and thus begin actively to follow his Way.

12. Holy Conversation

Holy conversation comprises good conversational skills coupled with content focused on the gospel. The rules of good conversation connect people together in love and respect and keep the conversation going over time. The content of holy conversation keeps that conversation focused on Jesus in all his many aspects. Our goal is be competent and knowledgeable conversationalists even as we trust God to work in the lives of our friends as well as in our own life.

NOTES FOR SMALL GROUP LEADERS

It isn't hard to lead a small group. Mostly what you have to do is initiate discussion by asking the questions, keep the group moving through the material at a good pace and end on time. What follows are brief suggestions that might make it easier for you to lead the group.

TASKS OF A SMALL GROUP LEADER

Preparing for the Session

1. Create a *comfortable setting* for the small group.

   - Put the chairs in a circle so everyone can see everyone else's eyes. (You can't have a real discussion unless you can speak directly to each other.)

   - Deal with potential distractions. Put the dog outside. Shut off the phone ringer. Ask people to turn off cell phones. Get a babysitter for the kids.

   - Have enough material (books, whatever you will use) for everyone.

   - Prepare the food (or make sure someone brings food).

2. Prepare to lead by carefully *going over the material* for the session.

   - Read through the two input sections so you have a good grasp of what is said and understand why it is being presented and how it feeds the group discussion.

   - Go over each question carefully. Think about how you might respond. Think about how others might respond and how you can encourage responses.

   - Be very clear about how much time you have for each section. Think about which questions you may want to drop if you run out of time.

Leading the Session

1. Beginning

   - Welcome people.

   - Open briefly in prayer, asking God to guide your discussion.

2. Life

   - Look at the "Story" section. See "How to Use the Holy Conversation Small Group Material" (pp. 18-21) for various ways to do this. Make sure the group grasps what is being said in this section.

   - Move to the first discussion section: "Life: How We Live It." The first question is always a relational question, that is, it asks people to share an experience. As leader it's your job not only to ask this question but to give the first answer.

- Go around the circle so each person gets a chance to respond.

- Ask the second question. This is an open discussion question, not a circle response question.

- Ask the third question if there is time.

- Be sure to end this section on time and then move to the next section.

3. Truth

- Once again, make sure the group has grasped the material in the "Concept" section.

- Have someone read aloud the "bottom line," which summarizes the main point.

- Work through the exercise or the questions in "Truth: How We Apply It."

- Discuss what group members are learning from their conversation partners.

- End this section on time.

4. Conclusion

- Remind people of the "Study" exercise and the material in "Resources" connected to this session.

- Encourage them to keep talking with their conversation partner.

- End with prayer.

FREQUENTLY ASKED QUESTIONS

1. *What is the purpose of question 1?*
The first question is always a relational question. It asks people to share a bit of their own story. The purpose of this question is to build trust (we grow to like those whose stories we know) and to establish the theme of the session via real life experiences. Often the responses to question 1 are the sorts of stories you can share in the course of holy conversation.

2. *Why does the small group leader have to be the first one to respond to question 1?*
You act as a model for how to answer a relational question. You do two things. First, you model an appropriate length of response. If you take five minutes to respond, you have just given tacit permission to the other group members to take at least five minutes to respond. This means you won't begin to get through all the material in the session since the bulk of the time has been spent on the first question. So respond in a minute or less. Second, you model an appropriate level of openness and honesty in sharing and so encourage others to be candid.

3. *Sometimes a single question has several parts to it. Do I ask the first part of the question and let the group discuss it and then move on to part two of the question?*
No, read the whole question at once with all its parts. When questions are clustered together they all revolve around a central theme. Different people will respond to different parts of the question.

4. *Is it necessary to have food at each session?*

No, you can do a small group without feeding people. However, food draws people together, especially if they are strangers. What you serve can be quite simple: snacks or even just soft drinks. A potluck supper each week prior to the session is a wonderful experience. In any case, it is not necessary for the small group leader to arrange for food. Share the responsibility. Or give it over to someone who loves doing this.

5. *Why do I have to keep moving the group along? What if we get to a question that generates a lot of energy?*

First, you need to know that there will never be enough time for discussion. This is just the nature of a good small group. So use the time you have wisely. Don't worry about time you don't have. Second, certain questions tend to get people talking. This is especially true of history-giving questions in which people are asked to share stories from their lives. People like to tell stories. We like to hear stories. But stories can go on too long and eat up too much time. Third, each session is balanced between story and concept. It's easy to focus mainly on story to the exclusion of the concepts. But it's important to discuss the various aspects of the gospel. This is at the heart of learning to be a good conversationalist. So make sure you get to the content questions.

HOLY CONVERSATION

The Lost Art of Witness

[This article was first published in Word & World *22, no. 3 (2002): 255-63.]*

Spirituality is a topic of great interest in our society as we enter the twenty-first century. A vigorous conversation is going on around us about God, about the nature and meaning of life, about spiritual practices and about what it means to be a person open to both the natural and the supernatural sides of life.

A friend of mine, Barry Taylor, who is both a pastor and a professional musician, tells of a screening he attended of the film *The Third Miracle* (1999), directed by the talented Polish filmmaker Agnieszka Holland. Barry was the musical supervisor on the film in addition to writing several of the songs used in the film. This was a pre-release screening and its purpose was to test out a version of film before a live audience. At the end of the screening the producers tried to get feedback about the film, but all the audience wanted to do was talk about God. Despite the best efforts of the filmmakers, they could only sit back and listen to the energetic conversation by this largely secular audience about spirituality.

The interesting thing is that the church may or may not be invited to be part of this conversation. Those of us who are active in the Christian church would, at first glance, appear to be ideal conversation partners. After all, we are already commit-

ted to a religious way and therefore, presumably, have valuable input on the topic of spirituality. But the problem is that we committed Christians are suspect. We are suspect on two counts. First, by aligning ourselves with a church we are associating with organized religion, and while spirituality is in, religion is out. Institutions are understood to squash or limit exploration of spirituality by insisting that certain doctrines are true (and others are wrong) and by promoting certain ways of living (which limit personal freedom). Second, religious people bring an agenda to the conversation. We seek the conversion of others. While our concern may be well-intentioned, it is manipulative (or so it is felt). Who wants to talk to someone who thinks you need to be converted?

This is the challenge for concerned Christians who want to be part of this cultural conversation but who also want to be faithful to what we have come to know and experience in our Christian faith. How do we talk about faith in ways that are honest, accurate and genuine in the midst of a postmodern climate that is suspicious of truth claims, hesitant to make commitments that seem to limit personal freedom, and dismissive of institutions that appear to be self-serving? However, there is another side to postmodern reality. Postmodern people are actively searching for truth that is experiential, for communities in which that truth is lived out and for spiritual experiences that are real. So the challenge is to learn how to converse in ways that touch these longings, are faithful to core Christianity, and are noncoercive.

Mandate

During the first century Christians sought to share their faith in Jesus with those in their community. To talk about Jesus to others was to be a "witness." In Greek, *witness* is a legal term meaning attesting to the facts or asserting the truth. In Luke 24:48 Jesus commissions his disciples to be his witnesses. They are to bear witness to "Jesus as Messiah, the fulfillment of all the Scriptures in him, his suffering and death, his resurrection and the proclamation of repentance and faith in his name to all nations, beginning from Jerusalem."[1] The Greek word *witness* (root *martyreō*) is where the English word *martyr* is derived and as such points to the fact that at various times in history it was dangerous to attest to this particular set of truths.

This same call to be a witness is found in Colossians 4:5-6: "Be wise in the way you act toward outsiders; make the most of every opportunity. Let your conversation be always full of grace, seasoned with salt, so that you may know how to answer everyone." This is the final exhortation in Colossians, and it points out the concern that Paul and Timothy have that this community of Christians be in conversation with their non-Christian neighbors. They are called on to be "wise" in how they conduct themselves toward others.[2] They are to seize the opportunity whenever it presents itself to proclaim the gospel. (This phrase is filled with the Pauline sense of the eschatological imperative: the time is short until Christ returns again so they must "redeem the time.") Verse six "envisages a church in communication with those around it, not cut off in a 'holy huddle' speaking only 'the language of Zion' to insiders . . . but engaged in regular conversation with others, and in such a way as to allow plenty opportunity to bear testimony to their faith."[3] This conversation is to be gracious and attractive, one which "delights and charms." It is to be interesting and never bland or insipid. And the Christians should be able to respond wisely to questions concerning the faith.

The comments of James Dunn on verse six capture what is being envisioned by Paul and Timothy:

> This picture is as far as we can imagine from that of the Christian who has no interest in affairs outside those of faith or church and so no "small talk," no ability to maintain an interesting conversation. In contrast, it envisages opportunities for lively interchanges with non-Christians on topics and in a style which could be expected to find a positive

---

[1]Michael Green, *Evangelism in the Early Church* (Grand Rapids: Eerdmans, 1970), p. 71.

[2]The exhortation to "walk in wisdom" summarizes one of the main emphasis of the letter (see Colossians 1:9-10, 28; 2:3, 6-7, 23; 3:16). See James D. G. Dunn, *The Epistle to the Colossians and to Philemon* (Grand Rapids: Eerdmans, 1996), p. 265.

[3]Dunn, *Epistle to the Colossians*, p. 266.

resonance with the conversation partners. It would not be conversation which had 'gone bad,' but conversation which reflects the attractiveness of character displayed above all by Christ. Moreover, such advice envisages a group of Christians in a sufficiently positive relation with the surrounding community for such conversations to be natural, a group not fearful or threatened, but open to and in positive relationship with its neighbors. . . . Such conversations, however, would regularly and quite naturally throw up opportunities to bear more specific Christian witness—not as something artificially added on to a "secular" conversation, nor requiring a special language or manner of speaking, but as part of a typical exchange of opinions and ideas. . . . [I]t should be noted how integrated their faith was expected to be with their workaday lives in the city and how rounded the religion that could both charm a conversation partner by its quality and give testimony of faith as part of the same conversation."[4]

This is our challenge today: to be these kinds of conversation partners in the midst of a culture that is fascinated by spirituality. Yet the reality is that we are seldom as wise, as engaged, as interesting or as charming as those pictured by Paul and Timothy. Part of the problem is that we have not given much thought as to how to express our faith to those who do not

share that faith. Nor have we wrestled with what it means to listen to others who are exploring the spiritual way. The result is that when we venture into such areas, the outcome is often a muddled conversation, filled with extensive use of a theological vocabulary that both mystifies and confuses our conversation partners. The challenge, therefore, is to prepare ourselves to be fit and lively conversationalists. The church needs to become far more intentional about preparing people to be witnesses to Jesus Christ.

Witness

Nowadays in the North American context we are unlikely to be punished for being a witness. More likely, we are simply ignored, kept out of the conversation or judged to be a religious fanatic. What went wrong? How did witness gain such a notorious reputation?

Part of the problem has to do with how we have come to conceive of witness since World War II. The process of witnessing, it seems, has been reduced to three main elements: personal testimony, a plan of salvation, and a call to commitment. *Personal testimony* is the story of one's conversion experience. Such a story follows a familiar format beginning with an account of one's pre-Christian life (sometimes told in rather lurid detail), followed by the dual discovery that one is a sinner living apart from God and that Jesus is the way back to God (often a highly emotional discovery), and concluding with the decision to repent of one's sins and accept Jesus by faith as Lord

[4]Ibid., pp. 267-68.

and Savior. Interestingly, this story is generally told in ways that echo the apostle Paul's sudden conversion on the road to Damascus (a punctiliar event) even though the majority of committed Christians come to faith slowly over time (a process, not an event).[5] The aim of such a testimony is to describe the wonderful change that has taken place in the life of the Christian since conversion and thus generate interest on the part of the other party.

The *plan of salvation* (a half a dozen popular options are now circulating) is intended to provide information about how to meet Jesus, the motivation to do so and a method by which to respond. Salvation has been reduced to "accepting Jesus as Lord and Savior." The "sinner's prayer" by which this is accomplished is often stated in almost contractual terms. If I believe that Jesus died on the cross for my sins and if I ask him to forgive my sins and save me, I will receive eternal life.

Once a testimony is given and the plan of salvation outlined, the witness ends with an appeal to "decide now for Jesus." Such a *call to commitment* is based on the assumption that the person with whom you are speaking is at the point in his or her spiritual journey where it's possible, then and there, to make such a commitment. The challenge is often presented in stark terms: What if you were to die tonight, would you be sure that you would go to heaven?[6] At other times the emphasis is on the significance of the moment: This may be the last chance you have to decide for Jesus. At still other times, the challenge echoes Pascal's wager: What do

you have to lose? Saying yes to Jesus will gain for you the free gift of eternal life.

It is necessary to critique this way of witness. On the positive side it has to be said that large numbers of people are now active Christians because of just such a challenge. Lives have been changed, people have been converted, and the church has grown because of this form of outreach. While this approach seems formulaic, at least it gives Christians something to say, a place to start and an understanding of the gospel. Furthermore, such evangelistic presentations stand in stark contrast to the bland conversations about religion some Christians have reluctantly engaged in, during which banalities are expressed, generalities are the order of the day and politeness is the inviolable atmosphere.

On the negative side, such forms of witness are mostly monologue, not dialogue. There is little opportunity for questions. In fact, training programs often discourage responding to questions, or they provide brief answers to "typical questions." Such answers are assumed to settle the matter so that people can get on to the real question, which is deciding for Jesus. In fact, these "answers" seldom do more than touch superficially on what are often issues of deep concern. Furthermore, there is a kind of mechanical feel to such gospel presentations, which is not unexpected given that people are encouraged to memorize a kind of script. In many cases the presentation is filled with theological language that is incomprehensible to anyone who has not grown up in a church. The result is that the gospel is half-understood (or grossly

---

[5]See Richard Peace, *Conversion in the New Testament* (Grand Rapids: Eerdmans, 1999), p. 286.
[6]See D. James Kennedy, *Evangelism Explosion* (Wheaton, Ill.: Tyndale House, 1970), p. 22.

misunderstood) by the recipients of the witness. How can you respond when what you know is so distorted? And the challenge to respond assumes you are able to respond, even though most people first have to wrestle with a host of issues before they can come to the point where they understand Jesus and his call in the context of their own lives.

The problem with conventionalized witness, apart from anything else, is that it is has become counterproductive. In our current cultural context people simply switch off when the conversation moves in a stereotypical direction. And this kind of witness has become stereotypical. The very success of parachurch organizations that train their followers in these ways of witnessing means that most everyone has heard this plan of salvation. It's old news.

Furthermore, witness of this sort is all about explanation. In this postmodern world, which has come to distrust metanarratives and truth with a capital T, few are convinced by finely crafted presentations. The witness that convinces is a life rich in spiritual experience in the context of a loving community that is the bearer of this story. Demonstration must precede explanation.

Conversation

In his study of the nature of conversation, Geoff Broughton concludes that genuine conversation is characterized by four factors: mutuality, reciprocity, openness and respect.[7] Perhaps this gives us the clue we need as we look for new ways to share our

faith with others. What might witness look like were it characterized by a mutuality that includes all partners in the conversation (over against monologue)? What might it look like if all the conversation partners were free to express their thoughts and experiences? What might it look like if there were an honesty that did not so much seek to present a party line as to share one's insights and experiences both positive and negative? What would witness be like if there were a profound respect for the uniqueness of each person's God-given life and experience?

What I am proposing is a much riskier proposition than simply laying a plan of salvation on an unsuspecting stranger. It will require deep trust in the work of the Holy Spirit. In the past it's almost as if we couldn't trust the Spirit. It was up to us to manipulate and maneuver the other person into the kingdom even though we gave lip service to the proposition that it is the Spirit who brings conviction to the hearts and minds of men and women. However, in what I am suggesting we would have to believe deeply in the work of the Holy Spirit because our role would simply be that of a witness in the original sense of the word: one who attests to the facts and asserts the truth. Our task would be to tell our story in the context of *the* story and then let happen what the Spirit makes happen.

Paradigm

Here is what I propose as a way to become genuine conversation partners with those

---

[7]Geoff Broughton, *Authentic Dialogue: Toward a Practical Theology of Conversation* (Th.M. thesis., Fuller Theological Seminary, 1998), p. 86.

who are exploring the nature of spirituality.

First, we need a *paradigm* that gives us the ability to talk with others about spiritual reality and remain true to who we are even while we are fully open to the uniqueness of others. I would propose that the concept of *spiritual pilgrimage* provides us with the perspective we need. At the heart of such a perspective are several assertions:

- All people are on a spiritual pilgrimage. We can't help it. This is how God made us. We are creatures in touch with both the natural and spiritual world. So everyone has a story to tell.

- Different people are at different points in their spiritual pilgrimages. Each person has his or her own issues and questions to wrestle with. Each person needs to be challenged to face these issues and move through them to new commitments.

- Those who have spent more time in conscious spiritual pilgrimage will probably have useful insights for newer pilgrims. Sharing our struggles and discoveries aids others in their journey.[8]

- Those who are committed Christians must feel free to own the particularity of their experience without the need to find a common spiritual consensus that will satisfy everyone. They need to be themselves with forthrightness, warmth, knowledge and vigor even as they allow others that same option. The truth of Christianity is often experienced first and then understood.

- Those who are active Christians are not simply the senior partners in the conversation. They too have their own issues to face. Pilgrimage is never finished. No one has mastered the spiritual life. More experienced pilgrims often grow by facing issues raised in conversation by those who have had radically different experiences of God.

- Exploration of issues of pilgrimage is probably best done in a community context. The collective wisdom of many is better than the single vision of one no matter how mature that person might be.

Second, there is the issue of the *content* of the conversations that might take place. The problem with the kind of dialogue that I have described is that most of us are bad at it. We know what we believe (sort of) and are okay talking about it in church with others who share our beliefs. There we can use a kind of code language together. We may not have a precise understanding of the theological terms we banter about, but we both know roughly what the terms signify. But move that conversation out into the marketplace and we are at sea. We find it difficult to translate the theological terms we use in church into words that are comprehensible at work. What we need is a new faith vocabulary: one that captures the essence of biblical terms in secular vocabulary. But this raises another problem. We are often not at all sure what actually constitutes the gospel. Beyond affirming our commitment to Jesus we have little to say. So it is hard to

---

[8]"The life of faith, the liveliness and the vitality of religion in our day, depends very centrally upon the stories we tell one another about our immediate encounters with an incarnate God" (Catherine M. Wallace, "Storytelling, Doctrine, and Spiritual Formation," *Anglican Theological Review* 81 [1999]: 49).

have a conversation with much depth when we as Christian witnesses are so muddled about our faith.

This is why, I think, that we have reverted to reductionist formulas to present our faith. At least we can memorize them and so we have something to say. However, when pushed, we have a difficult time amplifying the formula much less articulating its meaning.

The challenge to the church, of course, is to train its members in religious conversation. For the mainline church this means getting into a discussion of foundational doctrines. What do we mean when we repeat the Apostles' Creed each week? What are we saying when we assert that Jesus "was conceived by the Holy Ghost" or that on "the third day he rose from the dead?" This would be an enriching conversation for all involved, one that would pay rich dividends in terms of spiritual formation. For the conservative church this means getting beyond the assertion that "God loves us and has a wonderful plan for our life" or "we rebelled against God. Both actively and passively, we've all disobeyed Him. And our sins have separated us from Him, and broken off the relationship."[9] All of us need to learn how to talk about Jesus in ways that are accurate. We also need to know how to discuss the human condition, the nature of commitment and the dynamics of the spiritual life.

Third, there is the question of the *context* in which such conversations might take place. It's clear to me that the place

where such conversation can best thrive would in a small group. By a small group what I have in mind is a group of Christians and a group of seekers sitting around the living room and talking about their faith pilgrimages. When the rules of conversation are maintained (mutuality, reciprocity, openness and respect) the interaction will be rich and deep. In this context, the witness that takes place depends not on one person but flows from the whole group. Inputs of various sorts stimulate discussion, ranging from clips from contemporary films that display the human condition to study of the Bible with its wisdom about God. Over time the members of such a group will develop a deep trust and openness to one another and to God. In this context the aliveness of Jesus will become palpable.

Conversion

What about the outcome of such conversation? Wouldn't it be conversion? Conversion of each dialogue partner?

Conversion is a term that refers to change in which we leave behind one set of concepts, behaviors, attitudes and so on that we discover to be inadequate, ineffective, wrong or wicked. In their place we reach out to embrace a new, better, fuller, richer reality. Conversion to Jesus involves turning from sin (repentance) and reaching out (by faith) to Jesus. But conversion doesn't end with a single turning. As Christian pilgrims will testify, the turning

---

[9]The first quote is taken from "The Four Spiritual Laws" by Bill Bright, popularized by Campus Crusade for Christ. The second is from the so-called Bridge Illustration popularized by the Navigators, a parachurch organization. It is described in Mark Mittelberg and Bill Hybels, *Becoming a Contagious Christian* (Grand Rapids: Zondervan, 1994), p. 157.

to Jesus is just the first (albeit crucial) turning in the Christian life. The very process of sanctification involves multiple turnings as we seek ever better to be conformed to the image of Christ. And the dynamic by which we first embraced Jesus is the same dynamic by which we grow in the Christian life (repentance and faith).

This is *not* the conversion of just one conversation partner but both. This is what gives richness to this kind of conversation. There is no dominant partner; there are two or more individuals seeking growth and change (conversion). The imperialism of so much evangelism is done away with and replaced by the openness of all to the reality, power, and transformation of God.

At first glance, conversion and conversation are an odd pair. Apart from their similar sound, they seem to have little connection.[10] But it turns out that they are a fine pair. By conversation we are given the chance for conversion; by conversion we become open to new conversation in an ever-wider arena. Perhaps this is as it should be.[11]

---

[10]In fact there is an etymological connection between the two terms as is seen the history of the verb *converse*. In Latin, this term (*conversari*) means to "turn about with, hence to talk with," and the adjective (*converse*) is taken directly from *convertere*, conversus meaning conversion. So the idea of turning around one's life (as in conversion) has more than a superficial connection with turning around to talk to another (as in conversation). See Joseph T. Shipley, *Dictionary of Word Origins* (New York: Philosophical Library, 1945), p. 95. I am indebted to a student, Geoff Broughton, who points out this connection in his master's thesis, *Authentic Dialogue*, p. 5.

[11]I recommend several books, each from a quite different vantage point, that wrestle with the whole question of Christian witness. Rick Richardson's book *Evangelism Outside the Box* (Downers Grove, Ill.: InterVarsity Press, 2000) is written from the vantage point of a campus minister who understands well the postmodern mindset. In *How to Share Your Faith Without Being Offensive* (New York: Seabury, 1979) Joyce Neville struggles with the question of how Episcopalians can talk about faith issues.